GROWING WILD
ON EXMOOR

To Sheila and David Tucker

GROWING WILD ON EXMOOR

Molly Richards

ryelands

ACKNOWLEDGEMENTS

My thanks to Jenny Glanfield for her unstinting help and encouragement in getting my rather fragmented memories into book form. To Bill Warne for his beautiful photographs of Broomstreet. To John Gamlin, for letting me use an excerpt from his book "A Preliminary Survey of the Parish of Culbone". To my brother David and sister Josie for sharing and reinforcing some of my memories. To cousins and friends who have kindly lent me old photographs. And to Roland Vowles for kindly permitting me to reproduce some of his father's photographs in this book.

First published in Great Britain in 2007

British Library Cataloguing-in-Publication Data
A CIP record for this title is available from the British Library

ISBN 978 0 9556477 1 0

RYELANDS
Halsgrove House
Ryelands Industrial Estate
Bagley Road, Wellington
Somerset TA21 9PZ
T: 01823 653777
F: 01823 216796
email: sales@halsgrove.com
website: www.halsgrove.com

Printed and bound by
The Cromwell Press Ltd, Wiltshire

CONTENTS

Broomstreet, circa 1945.

Broomstreet in snow, 2005. ©Bill Warne

SHED

WALKING ON a new path, it occurred to me that being without my dog took so much pleasure away, made walking alone almost suspect, and me unable to relax enough to notice each turn of the lane and each new view.

The wooden shed stood close to the lane, unexpected here, where there seemed to be no access for motors. Further down, on a curve, I could see the corner of a stone built cottage, and behind trees, a chimney rising up, smoking.

The shed, its single door open, attracted me. I paused long enough to see if there was anyone around and seeing no one took a step inside. At once it all seemed so familiar, the old bench, a tatty armchair, a wooden ladder in the corner. The tools, saws, hammers, axes and two wooden planes were all set neatly against the side of the shed. There was an old pine table, stained and chipped, and on the table an empty mug with traces of dried cocoa.

And there was the smell. Each man's shed, it seems to me, has its own special smell, and this one, at last, had that same smell of sawdust, paraffin, paint and shoe polish that I had so often remembered from my grandfather Ridd's shed but had never since come across.

It was my job, when on holiday with my grandparents, to take Granfer's elevenses out to the shed where he would always be, mending something or cleaning the family shoes, arranging them in shining rows.

I had to make two journeys, as Granny would not trust me to take two cups of cocoa and six biscuits all at once. There were three plain biscuits for Granfer and three iced ones for me. I loved the little iced pictures of small houses, flowers and butterflies.

I had another look outside, there was still no one about, so I went in and sat in the armchair. It was surprisingly comfortable. I ran my hands along the worn and slightly greasy arms. Honest dirt, I could hear from some old wiseacre of my past.

Those few minutes I spent in someone else's shed had so much meaning for me. Here were memories of security, stability, of such happy interludes in my life. From somewhere came the words, biblical perhaps, that I should be as a little child – and I was.

After a few more minutes, I left the shed hurriedly, fearful of encountering anyone. I wanted to see no one. Not now. Memories had been stirred, some good, some bad, and I needed time to think.

ON THIS LAND

A FEW days later, I walked some of the fields at Broomstreet Farm. In my mind I heard some of those intense night time silences and then, in contrast, the wind blowing the great fir tree, and we children wondering if this was the night when it would come crashing down.

That great fir tree, in which by day we hid and spied, by night sheltered at least one barn owl. These birds could be seen sometimes in the evenings, white-faced and narrow-eyed, hunting low over the fields. Their weird shrieks could split the night awake and their snoring from the fir tree, presumably after a successful night's hunting, could even be heard in the house.

There was a tawny owl as well, more lovable than the barn owl, rounder, less ghostly, and sounding so lonely – whoo whoo oo oo – ending with a sharp, strong call of bequick.

How much nicer it was to have owls around the place, instead of pest officers and rat and mice poisons or traps...

I remembered the bats that we would try to bring down with a yard broom as they incessantly flew into our faces, and away again in a flash. We never got one. And the swallows' nests all around the farmhouse, with a continual, romantic twittering in the eaves. Then the line-up ready for departure and the beginning for me of autumn, my favourite season.

On this land, I have watched the ploughing and the sowing, the reaping and the mowing. Here in this very field, I have led the carthorse along the soft newly ploughed earth, nervously watching its heavy feathered foot being plonked down next to mine.

Bringing up a young family in the 1930s, as my parents did, must have been extremely hard, especially for someone of my father's temperament. There were no subsidies or guaranteed prices, and with meat and wool as expensive commodities, it was a time of extreme poverty for hill farmers.

In the tallet above the bull's house, I could often be found skulking away from arguments and impending clashes. I could pretend not to notice 'the wind getting up' as it were, yet be pretty certain of approaching rough weather.

From up there I could take a reading of what was happening below. By crouching down I could look through a foot-level window and spy on anyone crossing the yard. Hurrying hob-nailed boots striking at the cobbles (even making sparks fly if it was after dark), meant tempers had been lost: someone was leaving for ever, not going to take any more, had had enough.

My relief was great next morning to see whoever it was back at the breakfast table, albeit on the quiet side.

High up on the tallet wall someone had written with what looked like the wide flat writing from a carpenter's pencil:

Been busy planting cabbages all day
be glad when haymaking starts then perhaps
we'll get some cider or some beer
      yours truly
      Proper do cock

The message was there when our parents moved in to the farm in 1921, so it must have been put there for great-uncle John Red or even his father.

I knew that a 'proper-dough-bake' meant soft in the head, yet never, until now, did I make the connection between that and 'proper do cock'.

There were six of us children – David, Tom, Margaret, myself, Josie and Sheila – and we all had to help on the farm. We tied sheaves and stooked them, picked up potatoes and held the reins of horses in butts while mangolds were distributed to a flock of baa-ing sheep following behind. Then there was the icy coldness of the hurdling. Hurdling – a winter occupation – was moving the sheep hurdles each day to a new patch of roots. I cannot remember what important business made it necessary for small girls to be in attendance, but I think it must have been to stop the flock running through after the removal of the first hurdle.

We milked the cows, often before school, and sometimes after. We fed the chickens, collected the eggs, and fed the pigs.

There was no tractor on the farm then. The first one greeted with great enthusiasm by the men folk, was a Ferguson.

There was no telephone. If there was ever an emergency we ran to the next farm, Yenworthy, where Mrs French would let us make or receive a call.

At night came the filling with paraffin of the Tilleys, Aladdins and the feeble lantern throwing, not very far, a pleasing orangey pink glow as it swung through the farmyard.

Thinking of lanterns brings memories of times when all was well on the farm inside and out, and of the pleasure to be had from going out to the cowsheds and the stable. The chink-chink sound of cattle chains moving up and down the larch poles, when the cows were lying in their stalls, chewing and gently belching the night away, seen by the light of a swinging lantern, is a moment I hold in my heart for ever.

But then comes the contrast between that peaceful scene and the harsher reality of livestock farming. The cattle chains were necessary before the de-horning of cattle became common practice. My brother David remembers the absolute fear on the faces of cattle being driven willy-nilly all together into a shed, meaning that the aggressive beasts with long, sharp horns were able to pin the weaker animals to the wall.

I can still hear the constant distraught bawling at weaning time of ewe to lamb, cow to calf, which lasted, so my father said, no more than three days and three nights, but seemed much longer. Many a night I spent in agitation waiting for an end of it.

Perhaps for me the most hateful time was when the man came to kill the pig. I remember counting down the time to the end of the awful squealing, while I told myself that pigs squeal at anything and waited. Sheep go so quietly to the slaughter. I would go and look them in the eye, screaming in my mind, long before Dylan Thomas wrote a word: "Rage! Rage!"

Children do not see livestock as a commodity.

BROOMSTREET

BROOMSTREET FARM is situated equidistant between Porlock and Lynmouth, about 900 feet above sea level, with wonderful views north across the Bristol Channel to Wales.

The farmhouse, which is down a long lane leading off the A39 road, is an attractive, long, grey stone building with many pretty windows. In my mother's day, and subsequently my sister Margaret's, the garden was lovely, with lots of small trees and shrubs. My brother David, who lives there still, does his best to keep it in order, but he has limited time for gardening with so much else to do around the farm.

Numerous stone built farm buildings form a square of holding space, the main part of the square being taken up with a large old barn. Adjacent to the barn was a water wheel and on threshing days all used to be activity, noise and bustle, and the barn would be thick with dust. Three ponds in the combe above the farm fed the water wheel, which powered the threshing machine, the chaff cutter, the oat grinder, the circular saw and the bone grinder.

My great-uncle John Red, from whom my father took over Broomstreet, used to get his bones for bone meal sent down from Bristol and quite a proportion of these came from Bristol Zoo. The antediluvian bone crusher dealt with all that was fed into it until it was given the horns from an Exmoor horn sheep, at which stage it gave up the ghost and never crushed another bone. Its remains are still there in the garden as a decorative feature covered in moss!

Some of the bones, too, are buried about the farm and I'd like to be a fly on the wall one future day when the equivalent of today's Time Team come and unearth bits of lion, tiger and elephant on Exmoor.

Sadly, the water wheel is no more. My cousin Dick Gregory lived and worked with us during the war, because his sight was too bad for him to serve in the forces. He was a happy, relaxed sort of chap and we loved having him there. He threw everything into the war effort – including our lovely old water wheel!

Broomstreet is the middle farm of three. Yenworthy, to the west, is where my mother was born, and Silcombe, to the east, is where my father was born. The farms had two different landlords: Yenworthy belonged to the Halliday estate at Glenthorne, and Broomstreet and Silcombe to the Lovelace estate at Ashley Combe.

My parents married in 1920 and their very kind and obliging landlord decided to pension off great-uncle John Red and his sister Elizabeth, letting them retire to nearby Littlewood – now known as Twitchen – thereby freeing up the farm for the newly-weds. How lucky they were – a lovely farmhouse and some 350 acres of healthy, high, stock-rearing land.

I came on the scene in 1927, in the same bedroom as my two brothers and my sister Margaret were born, in a room with a view of the sea, and where in due course, Josephine Elizabeth and Sheila Nancy were also born. There is some question about the date of my birth: Mother insisted it was April 16th. However, Granny Ridd noted in her diary that I was born on April 18th.

There are two modest literary connections with Broomstreet and my family. One is the possibility that Coleridge might have been disturbed there by the infamous "person from Porlock" while he was writing *Kubla Khan*.

Coleridge's memory was apparently vague regarding place names and in a note appended to a draft manuscript copy of *Kubla Khan* discovered in 1934, the poet had written: "This fragment, with a good deal more, not recoverable, composed in a sort of Reverie brought on by two grains of Opium, taken to check a dysentery, at a Farm House between Porlock and Linton, a quarter of a mile from Culbone Church, in the fall of the year 1797."

This fuelled the assumption that the poem's place of birth was Ash Farm.

However, Coleridge himself is reported as stating, albeit thirty years after the event, "I wrote *Kubla Khan* in Brimstone Farm between Porlock and Ilfracombe – near Culbone."

I would be pleased if it were ever established that *Kubla Khan* was written at Broomstreet, but as that is most unlikely to happen, I am just as happy to know – and, in such a circumstance have more leisure to appreciate – that, when I walk in Culbone Woods, Coleridge and Dorothy and William Wordsworth also walked that path.

The second literary connection comes on my mother's side. Her maiden name was Ridd, but she and my Granny Ridd always disclaimed any connection with John Ridd, the hero of *Lorna Doone*, and disliked being questioned about it at a time when the novel was read more than it is today. I have every sympathy with them. Tourists used to come, in their latest country wear, to confront anyone they happened to meet on the farm with their "Do you think?"s and "Do you believe?"s and all the time the person being quizzed would be hopping from one foot to the other trying to get back to something real.

I cannot however help being intrigued by the suggestion made in John Gamlin's book *A Preliminary Survey of the former Parish of Culbone, West Somerset*, where he adds to the controversy regarding the location of Doone Valley. He writes:

"I would make a possible connection with Culbone of another famous literary work. It is often remarked how little resemblance 'Doone Valley', off Badgworthy Water, bears to the scenes described in R.D. Blackmore's novel 'Lorna Doone'. If you walk through Culbone Woods, pause where one of the streams plunges down the wooded hillside, and look up the course of the water, you will instantly recognise the scene depicted when the young John Ridd climbs up the waterfall prior to meeting Lorna in 'Doone Valley'. It is very probable that Blackmore walked Culbone Woods at some point in time, and I believe he may have transported what he saw to the location of his book as being better suited to the grandeur and excitement of his story."

In 1952, my parents were offered the chance to buy Broomstreet, when our landlords sold up part of the Ashley Combe estate. At the same time my uncles at Yearnor and Silcombe were also able to buy their farms. Now we were the owners instead of tenants and this felt good, yet despite the fact that my father was in the position of being able to do all the things which the "bloody landlords" had neglected to do, he never did any of them.

*My great-great-great grandparents,
Mary and Thomas Ridd, about 1860.*

*My great-grandfather Pile
(Granny Ridd's father).*

Helen Pile (Granny Ridd) aged 16.

*John Ridd (Granfer Ridd),
aged 14.*

GRANNY AND GRANFER RIDD

I SUPPOSE when thinking of grandparents most of us have one special one who meant more to us than the others. In my case it was Granfer Ridd. There was something about him utterly pleasant and agreeable. He was so calm. When you were with him you felt that he cared about you, and yet you knew it wasn't just you: in his mild and unassuming way, he seemed to like everyone.

There was no malice in him at all. Neither was there anything uncontrolled, nothing wildly exciting, no fireworks. I had enough of those at home. In a word, I found Granfer steadying. I was at ease with him and could chatter away to him endlessly and mindlessly. And, while I knew he was taking in every word, he carried on with whatever he was doing in his shed: reframing a picture, resoling a boot or shoe, with only an occasional little noise, not unlike a small cough, pitched in such a way that it always seemed to convey the right sympathetic response.

I, of course, was in my element, with an agreeable, agreeing captive audience of one.

Granny Ridd was good and kind, yet she somehow made me see myself in a bad light. I fell short of how a nice, well brought up little girl should behave. I believe she saw in my ways the ways of her errant son-in-law, my father. Margaret was her favourite granddaughter.

Granny Ridd's own life had not always been trouble free. As Helen Pile, she had been engaged to marry a local young farmer who, seeking to better himself, decided to go to New Zealand to get work on a farm and look around to buy a place for them to live in that wonderful country.

Helen was to wait until he returned, so that he could make his farewells to his family and get married in this country before they both left, spending their honeymoon on board ship.

This gave her time to think. She was part of a very close family, especially close to her mother, and the thought of leaving became harder and harder to bear.

She had also, to make matters even more complicated, come to be very attracted to John Ridd. Helen was in a fix. She had very high standards and the thought of befriending the one whilst being engaged to another would have very badly upset her. The trouble was, communications were very slow in those days, letters taking more than a month to reach New Zealand.

Her fiancé came home after three years and presumably she told him that she had changed her mind. In any event, I'm pleased to say that she married John Ridd, and they set up home at Yenworthy, the next farm to the west of Broomstreet.

People used to remark that Granny Ridd was a very good manager. I have some of her diaries and accounts books, which show that she and Granfer seem to have made a very good living. Taking 1916 as an example, her takings for the year came to £211.19.4d, which included lettings at Yenworthy, milk, cream, eggs, poultry, keeping of pony and carting. Each of the accounts mention carting, which I assume means fetching from and taking to the railway station at Lynton.

Granfer's takings for that same year came to £653.10.8d, which meant by my reckoning that Granny was able to invest almost a third of their joint income.

As well as letting rooms in their own house at Yenworthy and owning more property in Lynton, my grandparents bought four terraced cottages at Lynbridge. They also bought shares and war loan and war bonds. From Granny's records, they appear to have been moneylenders to family members needing a quick fix. The records also show that all such debts were repaid.

They could be quite generous and I suspect that their help, to a large extent, carried us through some of the worst patches of poverty during the Depression. How could they not have done? They had an unreliable son-in-law, with six children. Yet I feel sure that Granny Ridd would have carefully measured any help given, wanting my father to face his responsibilities. And I can see, too, his pain and belittlement, the hurt to his pride, in such handouts.

Their own children – that is my mother, Aunt Helen, and Uncle Tom – first attended the local school at Countisbury, and then went to a boarding school at Lynton. The girls duly progressed to a school with the most cringe-making title of Barnstaple Ladies School, run by two Miss Wrights. Uncle Tom went to Wallingbrook School at Chulmleigh.

In 1926, the year before I was born, my grandparents left Yenworthy and purchased Brendon Manor. The Manor lies about half a mile beyond the church, hidden in a little tree surrounded hollow. There was plenty of room for Granny to let some of her rooms to holidaymakers and those who could afford to brought their own maids and horses and grooms.

Randolph Churchill and the Mitford sisters came at one time to Brendon Manor for a holiday. Granny Ridd, although she was apparently rather dismissive of them, must have been captivated by such high spirits.

There was some land attached to the Manor and you could ride straight out on to the moor. Here, as at Yenworthy, I see from Granny's accounts that people seldom stayed less than two weeks and often came for months or even a whole season. The Manor is now run as a riding stables and the house divided into flats.

When my brother David was five years old he was sent to live at Brendon with our grandparents. This was principally because he was too young to walk all the way to Oare School on his own, whereas Brendon School was a little less than half a mile from the Manor. But no one took the time to explain to him properly why he had to go away to live, only returning home during the school holidays, and he felt very lonely and insecure. Having said that, I see the mark of Granny Ridd on David to this day: he has better manners and is much more considerate than the rest of us.

He returned home to live when he was seven, considered old enough now to take himself and Tom safely down to Oare School and back. He tells me that, very early on, they walked into the stag hunt in full cry. He was so alarmed that he took himself and Tom straight back to Broomstreet.

1911 Back row from left: Grandfather Richards, Irch Richards (bridegroom), Ada Richards (bride), Mr Woollacott. Front row: Grannie Richards and Mrs Woollacott.

Joe, John and Ilott Richards, 1919.

Granfer Ridd with Widow Fisher's great long gun (early 1920s) ©Alfred Vowles
"For happening to fire the ricks of a lonely farm called Yeanworthy, not far above Glenthorne, they approached the house to get people's goods, and to enjoy their terror. The master of the farm was lately dead, and had left, inside the clockcase, loaded, the great long gun, wherewith he had used to sport at the ducks and the geese on the shore. Now Widow Fisher took out this gun..."
Lorna Doone, Chapter 48

1921 John and Dick Red of Broomstreet.

18

GRANNIE RICHARDS

I NEVER knew my Grandfather Richards, because he died when my father was in his teens. Grannie Richards, however, was definitely a part of our lives.

When I was old enough to appreciate her no-nonsense personality, I began to notice that her nut-brown face, rosy cheeks and small stature carried a power that could very much intimidate my broad-shouldered, six-foot tall father, who was afraid of strong women and especially of appearing a failure in his mother's eyes.

I never saw her do a single domestic thing, not even wash a cup. She was very much an outdoors woman. In her black floral-sprigged long skirts, thick black stockings and always with a velvet neckband, she ran around the farm keeping a sharp look out. I say ran because that is what she did. She always had something in her hands, things she found lying around which she thought might come in useful or save a penny or two, like a few twigs or sticks, handy for lighting the fires, or a handful of wool found entangled on the fence, and often a toddler under her arm.

It was with sheep that she was an experienced and valued help. Her visits, especially at lambing time, could last a month. She also came to brew the beer for sheep shearing.

My brother Tom could attract a lot of Granny's ire. Perhaps she saw his potential as a sheep man, and perhaps she was aware too of something else that needed remedying.

During her long visits, my mother would give up to her mother-in-law the place she shared with my father at the head of the table. From there, Grannie would rule the roost, keeping a watchful eye on us all. Occasionally, she would leap to her feet, run round the table to where Tom was sitting, give him a sharp clip round the ear, saying as she went, "Cheeky little brassy!"

"What have I done?" Tom would mutter, putting on his most innocent face. None of us ever saw the looks that she alleged had passed between her and Tom. It seemed to be a kind of game they played, for Tom certainly very much admired Grannie and she thought highly of him.

Josie became her favourite girl in the family. Josie would not baulk at the messier bits of farming and would happily carry newborn lambs covered in yawk (yolk), messy yellow stuff which Margaret, Sheila and

I found too yucky for words. However at Grannie times it had to be done: it would never have occurred to any of us to not obey her.

When she had to get the sheep from one field to another, and where the lane diverged, it was not unheard of, there being no other help available, for Grannie to plonk a baby too small to toddle off in the middle of the lane, to stop the sheep going that way.

Because she was so much better a sheep farmer than my father, her effect on him meant his own mother temporarily taking charge over his territory. When he could no longer bear what he felt to be Grannie's critical view of his farming – and sustained already with a few nervers I expect – he would go all day AWOL. He would be shaky and sheepish next day and Grannie in a warlike mood. "Don't you bide sitting about in here," she would scold, "get out and look to the yaws."

And, hangdog as only my father could sometimes look, he went.

It was difficult to gauge how my mother felt about Grannie's visits. Pleased to see her come and pleased to see her go, I suspect. Grannie's strong and superstitious views on life were a bit wearing. She was fearful of many unseen things. The very idea of my mother refusing to buy from the gypsies who came annually to the farm threw her into panic. Perhaps Grannie was right, the reason for my mother's aversion to gypsies being that they beat up her brother Tom at Bampton Pony Fair, because he had turned their ponies out from his land where they were overnighted without permission.

So each year the gypsies came and we girls would gather round, despite my mother's efforts to keep us inside and away from them. She knew how they would flatter and tempt us with their gewgaws. Even as our mother was protesting that there was nothing she wanted this time, the whole caboodle would be spread out before us. Pillow slips, towels, sheets: "Pure Egyptian cotton, mum," or "'tis 'Orrockses, Mum."

It was Grannie's superstition that persuaded my father to purchase a goat to run with his cattle when they had an outbreak of brucellosis. He did it with a bit of embarrassment, saying that of course he did not believe in such mumbo-jumbo.

But Grannie Richards believed in many strange things.

In my mind's eye, I can still see her walking through the fields, a lamb in each hand, followed by bleating anxious ewes.

OUR-FATHER-WHICH-ART

OUR FATHER was born at Silcombe, the youngest son of a family of six. The only girl, our aunt Ilott, married into the Gregorys, a farming family near Taunton. Two of the five brothers, Joe and John, went to farm in New Zealand, leaving Irch (Richard), Herbert and Ernest at Silcombe. Irch was able to get the tenancy of Yearnor when he married Ada Woollacott, then Herbert married Ada's sister Annie and, as his own father had died, the tenancy of Silcombe passed to him. His widowed mother (our Grannie Richards) went to live with her daughter Ilott, spending many months of each year with one or other of her three sons – keeping her daughters-in-law and grandchildren in order too. It must have been very pleasant for the two sisters not only to be related by marriage, but also to be next door farming neighbours.

Ernest, our father, had by now decided that the one he wanted to marry was Mary-Char Ridd, who lived just two farms away to the west, at Yenworthy. They were married in 1921 at Oare Church and duly moved into Broomstreet Farm.

My father, with my brothers, my sister Margaret, and many other local people took part as extras in the filming of *Lorna Doone*. This was all of seventy years ago and I sulked for days because I was not allowed to go with them.

He was as dark as my mother was fair. Later, when I saw the stills photograph and eventually the film, I was somewhat shaken to see that he looked more like my idea of Carver Doone than did the actor playing the part.

Other people liked to be in his company. He was amusing, witty and on the generous side away from home. He was locally known as Farmer Ern, Uncle Ernest, or just plain Ernest by others, not often as Mr Richards, except by travellers in sheep dip or some such. Many travellers were a bit scared of calling at Broomstreet, for he was not an easy man to sell to.

We did as we were told all right when Father issued orders. Around the age of eight or nine I began to refer to him, in his absence, as our-father-which-art, showing a measure of affection and a measure of my belief that he knew what was best for us and should therefore be given respect. But there was also a growing sense of other emotions: being afraid of the cliff-edge atmosphere and the uncertainty in our lives.

It was at around the same age that I overheard one of my brothers saying to the other: "If the silly beggar didn't drink so much, it wouldn't be so bad." I had had no idea that my father's many changing moods and faces were all the result of heavy drinking, or indeed, of any drinking of alcohol at all. Until then he had just appeared absurdly happy or deeply pessimistic or downright nasty. Now, suddenly, it all made sense. And so began my increasing contempt for any man who could inflict such misery upon his family.

Everything was in the power of his voice, his vocabulary of frightening words, and his irrefutable presence. Our fear was of tipping him over into another drinking bout, to the anguish of our mother, the worry of the money spent, the arguments and the sheer exhaustion of having an alcoholic husband and six children to cope with.

I became aware around this time, that I was the member of the family most like him. I had heard my mother say to me, especially if I had done something she disapproved of, "Oh go away, you are exactly like your father." So there I was, stuck genetically to a father I could not admire. Yet I knew the movements of his hands – I make them – and I could sense his guilts, his hopes and his despair.

Between bouts of drinking he would be abjectly penitent. That was when I despised him the most. Too often we had heard the excuses and seen him in this apologetic state. We no longer believed him.

There would be days, a week perhaps, when he would stay around looking so miserable that I longed for him to go away again. I no longer knew what was normal for him, and neither, I believe did he.

Yet there was an upside to this. When in his cups, he was given at times to quoting from the Bible, according to his mood of the day. This was his repentant one: "We are none of us perfect, no, not one." This was often thrown over his shoulder as he passed through. Then there was his very sad and mournful quotation, which appeals to my wry humour. We were, after all, a household of six females and would often gang up against him. "Man that is born of woman hath but a short time to live." By this, I think he was implying that man born of man might have had a much better time of it.

He was a worrier par excellence, driving himself frantic over things that had not yet happened, nor were they likely to. The cynical view, which I often took, was that the worries were manufactured to give him another excuse to take to the bottle. However, when something serious happened he would sober up, taking the attitude, "It's happened now and there's nothing to be done."

He worshipped and resented my mother. He resented her for having six children and he resented her for having standards he could not reach. He resented his farming brothers for achieving so much more than he could. He eventually resented his own sons for their youth, their strong bond with their mother, and for the fact that his way of life depended on their cheap labour.

He resented his daughters for marrying the wrong men. He especially resented me for disregarding his command that "no daughter of mine uses bad language in this house," for when occasion demanded it, I successfully challenged him expletive for expletive.

My father should have been there more often, for it was in his absences that we showed our true colours.

The table we sat at was a long one, boys one side, we girls the other, and it was from here that we traded insults in a war of words, girls versus boys. My mother tried to stop some of our more personal, painful jibes, but with our father away it was as if an energy was released in us all and to make up for our repression when he was at home we became extremely hurtful.

It seemed to be Tom, always bad-tempered at breakfast time, who would start us off. If it was Margaret's turn, Tom would mumble sulkily, shifting dramatically to the left or the right along the bench, that he "did not see why he had to sit opposite a maggot." This, a reference to her pallor and her name – we sometimes called her Maggie – always upset her, which was what the sadistic side of his nature needed. After more and more words were thrown with contempt across the table, they would both get up to leave, Tom looking smug and Margaret planning a revenge – which she usually got.

When it was my turn to be put in my place Tom would mention my nose, saying that it wasn't a nose, it was a snout. This was often followed by the observation that he didn't think he had ever seen anyone quite as ugly. I usually found an apt response, but this one had me floored, although there was no way I would let him see it. My jibes to him, I felt, were superior to his, mostly on intelligence or integrity, and I felt that here was plenty enough to get my teeth into.

I do not say that our side never started these wars of words and I do not say that on some level it was not found by me to be an outlet, too. I was aware that whatever horrible things were said, the real hurt usually went to Tom. At least that was and is my perception of the situation.

Tom could also draw quite good caricatures to pass around the table. They were recognisable, hurtful and always funny, provided you were not the one being lampooned.

Neither of my brothers married. I am sure they both would have liked to, and there were many chances. The trouble was that any money had all been used by my father. In farming it was necessary that the man was able to offer something substantial. Even if you could not afford to purchase the farm itself, you had to be able to buy the stock. And, of course, our upbringing did not inspire us with much confidence.

Pride and secrecy kept Tom from proposing. How do you confess that you haven't got a bean? They did try to leave. Tom wanted to go to New Zealand, where so many of our relatives went and made good, while David wanted to go into the navy.

It surprises me a bit that hard and tough as we considered ourselves to be, neither of my brothers could withstand our mother's desperate pleading that they must not leave.

She was determined to keep us all at home. I imagine she must have thought that of her four daughters at least three would marry quite quickly. Perhaps she also hoped that one might not, and that one would care for her sons, for it was of them that she thought mostly. In her world, men needed women to care for them. I honestly do not know if she ever visualised either of her sons marrying.

In the end it was resolved by each of us going our own way, while still living under the same roof. David found his salvation in a life devoted to always doing well whatever he took on. Tom decided to live for the day, which he did most successfully. Margaret, who was taken off for a few years during the war to work in a munitions factory, declared that rather than return home to live she would marry the first man who asked her. Luckily she met Fred, who was in the army, and they did fall in love. Josephine and Sheila "threw their hats over the hedge", Josie to get married and Sheila to emigrate to New Zealand.

To make things easier for our mother, Sheila told her that the immigration deal was that she would return to England within two years, if she found that she did not want to make a future there, although I knew that she had absolutely no intention of returning.

In 1965 my mother took herself off to New Zealand to visit her. I think she was hoping to persuade them to come home. But Sheila had put down roots with her husband, the kind and loyal David Tucker, who also came from Exmoor. And their roots now extend to grandchildren.

As for me, I followed Tom's example, living for the day, finally leaving Broomstreet at the age of 32.

But I am jumping ahead. Back to my father, I feel that something should be said in his defence and, in trying to do so, have come to the conclusion that he really had no control over his drinking. He was certainly a man who cared very much for his wife and children. When sober, he was a sensitive man, perhaps too sensitive to be able to bear the plight of his family, so he returned to the only escape he could find. But, I feel bound to say, his means of escape was pretty unforgivable really…

My parents' wedding at Oare Church in 1921
From left: Granfer Ridd, Granny Ridd, Aunt Helen, Mary-Char (my mother), Ernest Richards (my father), Mr Nichols (best man), Aunt Ilott Gregory, Uncle Tom Ridd, Grannie Richards (seated).

From Granny Ridd's diaries.

1899: John's father went to Barnstaple very late back the train blew over no one hurt.

The Life boat was taken by road from Lynmouth to Porlock.

Sunday March 9th Joyce Molland born.

Sunday April 9th Mary Charlotte Ridd born.

April 1924 Bought Brendon Manor for £1700.

1937 Sold Brendon Manor to Major Archer Sept 29th.

Built cottage at Lyndown and came here to live on September 22nd 1937.

OUR MOTHER

I LOOKED through Granny Ridd's diary to see what she had written on the day my mother was born and was quite surprised to see the terse entry on the 9th April 1899: "Baby born". Nothing else. Nothing about its sex, its weight, or the parents' delight. Looking on to find her christening on May 21st, I find: "Had the baby christened". Then there was a list of who was present, but no mention of what name had been chosen.

I do not know why so little attention was given to such an important happening as the birth of a first child. I had always been aware that Granny was in no way besotted with her grandchildren: indeed, she was efficient and businesslike in her dealings with most people. Yet in another notebook I have of hers she writes in such an embarrassingly sentimental manner that, in fairness to her, I cannot bring myself to quote from it here. A bit of a mystery...

My mother was, in fact, christened Mary Charlotte Ridd, which soon became Mary-Char. She was born on a Sunday and, as we all know, "The child that is born on the Sabbath Day is bonny and blithe and good and gay". That was very true of our mother. Photographs show her as looking extremely pretty, fit and happy, and in nature she was just the same.

As a young woman she was very popular and had many friends. She knew how to look after and value friendships and I suppose loyalty should go high, if not at the very top, of her attributes.

The contrast between her life before marriage and after was pretty pronounced. As a child, she had security, lots of love, and an excellent education. After her marriage she was always worried about money, with a husband very different in character from her own father.

One sad entry in her diary reads: "Took to the bank thirty pounds two shillings and eleven pence. Paid Fulford Philips thirty pounds." This was an agricultural bill, so she was paying for the running of the farm, as well as housekeeping. At least she had a surplus of two shillings and eleven pence to use, but it somehow seems to sum up the whole of her married life and I still cannot read it without getting upset.

We all loved her with a great and painful love, and hated having to witness how our father treated her, particularly during his drinking bouts. The hurt he inflicted was in the degradation, the poverty, his rages and his mercurial changes of mood. There were so many little discomfitures. For instance, we used to see her hiding any bills that came into the house, until a suitable time came to show them to our father. And how many 'hidden' bottles did we find and pour down the sink? How soon into her married life did she have to learn such little tricks? I used to feel so humiliated for her. There were so many apologies and restarts – and so many failures…

Despite my father's shortcomings, it has to be said that he loved her and she was certainly 'an helpmeet' to him. A very good cook, she also loved gardening, and produced for him, much to his alarm and despair, six healthy children.

She would not tolerate any of us telling tales of each other's misdeeds. I remember Margaret rushing in to the house shouting "Mumma, Mumma, Tommy did paup," and my mother replying, "No, Tommy did not," and Margaret saying, "Yes, he did, *and* he did it on purpose!"

My mother's absent-minded reply to this, the same for every circumstance – even, I felt, murder – was, "Go away, you're a naughty little girl. I just know Tommy would never do that."

Every night we were made to say our prayers. You always knew your standing with my mother by the number of prayer books you collected. Some of us got none, Tom had quite a few.

How I wish that she had kept in closer touch with all her church-going friends. There was always so much to do and so little time to spend on anything outside the farm and family. The fashionable way to socialise in those days was to chatter over afternoon tea, but I cannot see my mother considering that a very high priority.

This reminds me of a little verse she sometimes used to quote:
"How very nice it is to see
Our dear relations come to tea.
How very nice it is to know
That when they've had their tea, they'll go."

Poultry was her great pleasure and contribution to the nearly always empty family coffers. During the war she was sending hundreds of eggs a week to the packing station. The incubator was placed in the outside loo: it was so good to sit watching the eggs warming and then the fluffy little chicks pecking their way out of the shell.

When my mother inherited some money in the late 1940s, it was put into the farm, partly in the form of a small herd of Galloway cattle.

Taking a short and rare holiday, she and my father, together with his brother Herbert and his wife Annie, from Silcombe, travelled up to Scotland, where they bought ten Galloway cows and a bull. There was great excitement when these duly arrived at Minehead Station.

My father and Uncle Herbert were co-tenants of Porlock Common,

From Granny Ridd's diaries.

1920: *April 6th Owen Sanders & Ada Mary Pile married.*

April 7 Mr Beard and Alice Ridd married.

Had Mr and Mrs Wellman and their French maid.

1921: *March 30th Mary wedding day.*

Brendon Manor

1926: *Mrs Abbott and party came July 15 to Sept 15.*

Mrs Bradford Brown came Sept 15 to Oct 13th.

1927: *April 18 Molly Richards born.*

26 David Richards came here to go to Brendon School.

July 8 Lorna Jean Ridd born.

21 Helen went to Broomst as they are all down with measles.

28 Mrs Abbott and party came.

August 9th Helen came home from Broomstreet with measles.

which was owned by the Blathwayts, and it was my mother's aim to run her Galloways up there.

I do not know how long it took her realise that she had bought badly. A law had come into effect in Scotland, whereby all cattle reacting to a TB test had to be destroyed. It was not until this test became compulsory in England that she discovered she had four reactors amongst her herd. She received compensation but this did not make up for the inconvenience and work involved in bringing wild cattle down from the moor each to be tested, and until the herd was clear, neither they nor their calves nor meat could be moved or sold.

Having the run of a common has always been a most prized asset for any hill farmer and one of the many grudges I carry against my father is that he let go his valuable share of the tenancy of Porlock Common. When the tenancy came up for renewal – agreements were made for least ten years in advance, maybe even longer – Uncle Herbert became concerned that they should get the next agreement to include their sons. My financially embarrassed father was not interested in this and so lost our family any rights on Porlock Common, which now goes in its entirety to Silcombe.

I was about eight or nine when we became the proud owners of a second hand Morris. Until then, most of our travel was on horseback. We children had ponies and there was a pony and trap, which was used mostly by my mother to take her and the produce to market.

My mother drove the car, my father realising perhaps that the Morris would have a short life, but a merry one, with him driving. In many ways this was a mistake, for now my mother was forever at his beck and call, and of calls there were many.

Once she refused to drive him somewhere and he promptly set off on his own – slap bang into the nearest wall.

With the car she had found a means of escape when my father was too intolerable, so he set about learning more of the engine and found that without the rotor arm, easily removable, the car would not start.

My mother, furious and frustrated, went to the local garage and got some spares. I still enjoy the memory of seeing the smile wiped off my father's face, when smug and smiling he produced the rotor arm from his pocket and showed it to us children, saying "Your mother thinks she's leaving, but I've got this!"

From the kitchen window we could see where the road went up and away with Ma in her car whizzing around the corner. How we hoped it was not forever. It never was.

CHARLIE AND LOUIE

I DO not remember a time before Charlie or before Louie, both of whom became immensely important in our lives, certainly in mine.

Charlie was from a local family but lived with us. He was very much an observer of life, not at all excitable, given to short, sharp, dry comments, often about our father, or the Sages in the farm cottage.

He had, too, a romantic side. We children would be given a few sweets or a penny or two to go and pick flowers for his girl friend who lived and worked at Oareford farm. He looked so smart when he set off, after dark, not wanting to be seen carrying his bouquet, I suspect.

When he became noticeably unhappy and the break up of his love affair came to light, I was quite perplexed and could not imagine any sane woman rejecting Charlie. He was kind, good looking, dependable. To my mind, in those days, he possessed all the qualities required for a happy marriage.

It was Charlie who, when my brothers, David and Tom were growing up, was always on hand to show them and teach them anything they were not familiar with. He was always there, a kind, decent, knowledgeable man. The irony of this, as he would have known, was that he was working his way out of a job. When the time came that my father thought David and Tom capable of coping, with just another less experienced lad around the place, and not needing the same wage as Charlie with all his knowledge and know-how, Charlie was given notice to leave. I don't suppose it came as a surprise.

Louie had been a Dr. Barnardo's child, given to them when her own mother died, and a stepmother came on the scene. She didn't talk too much about those years, but when I was out with her once we met a group of Barnardo's children and she quietly bought them all an ice cream. There was nothing showy or fake about Louie.

She came to Broomstreet from Yearner farm, where she had been working from the age of fourteen for my Aunt Ada, and became as family with us. What an erroneously cosy picture that paints. As family, working from daylight to dark. As family, very little pay. As family, few days off. After all, why would you want days off, when you are working for your own ends?

But Louie was not working towards her own better future. She loved children and must have hoped for a happier life. But there were no marriageable young men for her to meet.

Mary-Char Ridd, about 1905.

Mary-Char Ridd (my mother) 1916.

My mother, circa 1922.

My parents, circa 1924.

I did harbour a secret hope that Louie and Charlie might fall in love, a condition with which I became quite familiar once I was able to sneak a read of Louie's magazines and her Ethel M. Dell novels, which our mother had forbidden her to let us get our hands on. But this dream went unfulfilled.

Louie became a kind of surrogate mother to us, as her jobs were mostly domestic. Oddly enough I do not recall her ever cooking anything, although she must have done. I seem to remember her forever cleaning floors, furniture, brass candlesticks, plated silver teapots, cutlery, boots and shoes, and all sorts of silly and unnecessary gewgaws. Poor Louie. Mother much preferred being out gardening or seeing to the poultry – the fattening geese and ducks, the chickens and hens – and, of course, the cooking. Josie is the one of us most like Mother, but with no Louie to help her.

After our grandparents moved from Yenworthy to Brendon Manor, we would all go there for a mandatory Christmas visit. My mother would make her way there in the pony and trap, with a baby and perhaps Margaret. Upon arrival the baby would be fed, admired and put to bed in the bottom drawer of the chest of drawers.

Meanwhile, poor Louie would be in charge of the rest of us. In every kind of weather, she would lead the ponies with one or two children aboard, over the moor, up hill and down dale, and the rest straggling along on foot, all of us cold and complaining.

As with Charlie so with Louie, with four daughters in line to all be at home, Louie naturally had to go. She went to my Aunt Helen where there would have been less to do, and since Aunt Helen was my mother's sister, she knew and we knew that she wasn't lost to us for ever.

One year we girls wanted to go to Barnstaple Fair and there was a coach going from Brendon. My mother would only let us go if Louie went too, to keep an eye on us. While we were there, we had to try all the fairground swings and roundabouts and at one time Louie felt ill, but she soldiered on for our sakes.

She was not at all well on the coach back. The next day she spent in bed, and the next. The doctor was sent for. Three days later, she was lying dead in a Barnstaple hospital, having suffered a heart attack.

She had always had a high colour, so it is possible that heart trouble ran in her family, which was why her own mother had died so young. That we shall never know.

The funeral took place at Brendon church on 5th October 1945 and after all those years in which we thought we knew her, Louie had died at the age of 37 years.

When Aunt Helen went through her belongings she found six hundred pounds that she had saved, a considerable amount in those days. In order to try and trace Louie's family, Aunt Helen contacted Barnardo's and the Salvation Army, but with no immediate success. Then, one day, Louie's father turned up out of the blue. Aunt Helen said he was only in the house for ten minutes, leaving as soon as he had Louie's heart-breaking savings. He showed no interest at all in how she had spent her life, the manner of her death or where she was buried.

OARE SCHOOL

MY FIRST school was up the Oare valley, way above the church, above Oareford farm. There was a small cottage on the right of the school building, with a small garden at the front and, as a small child, I thought it huge and full of boisterous children. The pupils, in fact, numbered between nine and eleven, and ranged in age from David at ten and me at five.

If I were asked what single thing has improved for schoolgirls since I was a child, high on the list would come trousers. Imagine winter mornings getting girls ready for school. Woe betide the one who forgot to put the buttonhook back on its nail at the back of the door. Little girls wore gaiters, which had buttons all the way down the outside of each leg. Each of these twenty or so buttons was so trickily small that a child had to be a good age before managing to do this unaided. After buttonhooks and spectacles had been found, the open gaiters would be wrapped around the legs, held carefully in place by the child, the elastic fitted under the arch of the foot, over the boots or shoes, the flap of the gaiter placed over the lace holes, then the buttoning began. They were blissfully comfortable, but, oh, the palaver!

Any lack of discipline in our family came from rather too much control at home, so, as my mother would often tell me, away from home we could sometimes behave like little savages.

Perhaps you can imagine our delight at being befriended at the school by Jack, who had had no discipline at all. "I bungoin' do it," was his usual response to orders from above, and my awe and admiration of him was boundless.

We had one gentle teacher, Scottish I believe, called Miss Allen, who was so out of her depth, and quite unable to cope with our oafishness. Even now, I remember feeling for her an odd mixture of love and pity. She did after all teach me to dance the Keel Row – over a broomstick, for some reason – and it was from her that I got my first glimmerings of making some sense of the alphabet. I can still recall the excitement of constructing a simple sentence – the cat sat on the mat.

Once, I got the cane, for shouting in the playground, "Miss Allen loves farmer Dallyn." As farmer Dallyn often did odd jobs around the school house and garden, and as Miss Allen was unmarried, I suppose the older boys thought that the most likely scenario, so I was challenged to shout this out whenever he appeared.

My caning was so gentle that I enjoyed the limelight and my brief moment of fame. But as such punishments were usually doled out to the lot of us, standing in a line and holding our hands out, perhaps a tolerant affectionate amusement would best describe our feeling. After all, it didn't hurt and by now we knew who was in charge and his name was Jack.

We, as most country children then, had a very long walk to school. It was arduous, too, up through steep fields, then the joy of reaching the top and the happy downhill stretch through scratchy heather and gorse. I can still recall my horror, on my first day at Oare School, when I realised that the journey must all be done again in reverse to get home.

We were docile and attentive enough at lessons when there was nothing more exciting to do. The more exciting thing to do often took place after the sound of the hunting horn. There was nothing wrong with our hearing, and no matter how distant, led by Jack, without a backward glance, we were off, out of the door and half way up the steep before Miss Allen collected her wits.

If there was hunting to join, Jack went. As a fireman goes to a fire, so Jack went hunting. All his family always had and it would never have occurred to Jack not to.

I see Miss Allen now, on her small patch, ringing the school bell, calling plaintively, "Come back, children, come back all the lot", as if we were a multitude instead of a handful of very naughty children. We did not come back until the hunt had moved on, meaning that we were sometimes away from the school for an hour or more, then we filed back, holding out our hands for the cane. Not all the children left the classroom; three or four well-behaved ones remained, aware of the outcome of such goings on. We treated them with a scorn they did not really deserve.

We sometimes caught sight of the quarry, a fox or a deer. The boys got very excited, and yes, I did too, but mostly I liked the horses, their hooves beating on the heather, the colourful fearless riders in their red coats, and the sound of the hunting horn. It seemed so right, so what should be in a country landscape, as portrayed in all those sporting prints by Aldins and Edwards, which hung in so many Exmoor houses.

On our way home from school, the boys would occasionally stop at the river to tickle trout. They tried to get Margaret to try her luck, but she said no, we might tickle a snake instead. She knew such things could happen as she had heard our father telling the story. Then I too recalled the tale and could not be induced to have a go. Anyway, there was no point. The only fish we liked were Porlock Weir herrings.

There was a copse at the top of the hill where we would stop for breath, climb a few trees and generally mess about. Sometimes Jack would go that far with us, having no one to play with in the valley. That was where I became initiated into the gang. No one called it that, but in retrospect, I see it as the time I became accepted as more than the whining baby, the nuisance, and the hanger on.

After much whispering, they all climbed a big beech tree telling me to clear off, keep out of the way. I watched them go high into the tree, then all climb out on a single branch, further and further along it they crept, the branch falling lower and lower to ground. I was then called to come and help bring it down. "Whatever you do, don't let go," they said, and of course, so saying they all leapt off and I went flying through the air, somersaulting a couple of times and very luckily landing back in the tree, unhurt and amazed. I believe they were a little bit alarmed themselves, and for a while treated me with respect.

Concerned parents eventually got the school closed: there were too few pupils, and the ones they had were in need of a sterner teacher than Miss Allen. I think my description of us as being oafish was a bit too strong, in fact we were pretty standard and not ever to be described as young thugs. I doubt I was there as long as a year before the school was closed, and I feel that the time must have been what might be called today character-forming, and yes, I can visualise the odd wry smile.

WINDWHISTLE

I was young then, when great winds
bustled about my childhood home.
slavering wolves rattling at windows,
claw clicks on glass.

Slates from the roof
shattering to the cobbles below.

The cows chained in their stalls, open
to the icy winds, which rattled the corn bin,
blew away their bedding, and disturbed the bull.

Farm dogs at the end of the walkway
shivered and whined.

At dawn the wind dropped to a low growl
passing softly about the buildings
before flattening a path over Windwhistle Hill
where we walked in the fresh new morning air
reluctantly to school.

Circa 1913 Harvest Home at Oareford. ©Alfred Vowles

Oare Harvest Home. ©Alfred Vowles

1913 Oare Harvest Home. ©Alfred Vowles

OARE CHURCH

FOR AT least eight hundred years St Mary the Virgin, Oare, has been a parish church, while Oare itself is mentioned in the Doomsday Book as a village of some significance.

Oare sprang to fame when Richard Doddridge Blackmore wrote *Lorna Doone* in 1869. His grandfather, John Blackmore, was Rector of Oare from 1809 to 1842, so it was a countryside with which R D Blackmore was well familiar. He also had access to the parish records and knew of the notorious band of brigands who had taken refuge in the Badgworthy valley in the 17th century. From these facts he created one of the best-selling novels in modern literature.

Oare was the nearest church to Yenworthy, where my mother grew up and she loved it, always wanting to be part of whatever was happening there. For years she was the organist, and was very proud of her presentation clock when she left. I presume that it was because of getting married and all of us, that she gave up being organist and many of the services she would have liked to attend. There must have been many times when she very much needed the comfort of church in the following years.

This is my mother's account of harvest thanksgivings at Oare and Culbone churches. She wrote this when she was in her late eighties, after I asked her to put down some of her memories. Unfortunately, this was as far as she got.

"We had a united harvest thanksgiving with our twin parish. We always did everything together, except for the service, when ours (at Oare) was in the afternoon one Sunday and our twin (at Culbone) would have their service on the following Sunday. The churches were all beautifully decorated, the bells would ring and people would pour in as soon as the bells started, all in their best clothes, little girls in white dresses. Someone would be sent to borrow chairs from the nearest cottage. We had a very good service, with all the old harvest hymns – We *plough the fields and scatter* and *Come, ye thankful people, come.*

"We were lucky to have a very nice rector, who was good very sympathetic to anyone in trouble.

"Then, about a week after, the two parishes joined on a day of sport and merrymaking at a farm where there was plenty of room in a large field, as well as a large barn. There were sports for children, a long distance race for the men, pole jumping and a tug of war between the two parishes.

"The fun went on for hours. One man played the accordion with lovely dance music, and anyone who could sing sang along with such songs as *The Charge of the Light Brigade* and *The Village Pump*."

So far as we children were concerned, going to a church service was reserved for those days when we could be accompanied by a parent, usually our mother. On most other Sundays we attended Sunday school at Oare, except when the weather was too bad for us to go over the moor. The journey to the church was further than the one to the school, but again it meant going up the stony lane and through the steep fields. We never minded the downhill stretch, where we could run or roll all the way to the bottom, if we wanted, and there before us was the church.

I soon became quite a little believer, hardly grumbling at all at going and treasuring my little blue stamp book with a picture on the cover of Jesus as a shepherd sitting among his lambs against a purplish background, which I believed to be heather.

We children sat in a row, booted and gaitered legs dangling, most feet not making it all the way to the floor. The church – so cold in winter, so blessedly cool in the summer – bored me out of my mind and I remember nothing of the various clergy who came to give us religious instruction.

I used to long for something stirring to happen, fantasising that maybe a present-day Carver Doone would poke his gun through that same gunshot hole and fire off a round or two. It never happened, so all I could wait for was the moment when we were handed out our stamps with little biblical pictures on them, either to stick in there and then, or, if we'd forgotten our stamp book, to take home.

It was on the way home one Sunday, when half way up the hill I discovered that I'd lost my stamp. After I had made a great fuss, Tom, who hated walking as much as I did, lost his temper and turned on me, saying what did a silly stamp matter, and there was no such thing as God, and Jesus never existed, and if he did he was no shepherd, sitting around on a bank cuddling lambs, and in white clothes too, he snorted. As Tom turned out to be a born shepherd, you could sympathise. Then, though, it was an awful thing to say, and I was quite sure we would be struck by lightening on the way home. As we were not struck down I began to give serious consideration to Tom's blasphemy.

Sunday school was never the same again.

CULBONE CHURCH

CULBONE CHURCH, reputed to be the smallest complete parish church in England, gives off a very special feeling of peace and "all's right with the world", but the atmosphere is also quietly serious. The little graveyard seems to wait and listen as I do now, to the waves from the beach below crashing onto rock, and the trees shifting easily, swaying this way and that so that you are not sure if what you are hearing is the little stream, the sea or the trees.

It is a fantasy church in a fantasy setting.

"Sure was never a spot better calculated for the indulgence of the meditative faculty than Culbone church yard. Every circumstance around leads the mind to thought, and soothes the bosom to tranquillity." So wrote Warner in his walk through some of the Western Counties in the 1800s.

Culbone is the nearest church to Silcombe, where my father was born, and he would complain from time to time that it was *his* church, so why did we usually go to Oare? As even then both churches were run by the same reverend gentleman, my mother didn't think it should make much difference. For me, though, it did: I always preferred Culbone.

The very gravestones at Culbone were of more interest, many belonging to my ancestors, and in the vicinity there were real living cousins I could relate to, unlike at Oare where we seldom saw more than the elderly relation or the odd distant cousin twice removed.

And the walk to that church was to be looked forward to. We could either go over the fields and drop down just beyond Littlewood, and then walk the lovely path under Silcombe or we could go along the lane to Silcombe and down through their orchard.

Passing along the wintry lane when every stone and faded leaf would be edged with icy crystals, one or the other of us would always be left behind studying some winter beetle or loitering at the side of one of the many little streams that ran down the steep combes. There was Twitchen Combe, Silcombe and Holmers Combe to be passed on the way; each one fascinating and tempting for a good time-wasting, ice-breaking, feet-wetting loiter. Those in front would fall behind, those behind would overtake only to be passed themselves in due course. We did though arrive all together at the gate to Tom and Liz Cook's vegetable garden and – looking a little way beyond and below – there was the small church steeple.

And there, above the church, stood the pretty stone cottage, with its wide gateway, almost astride the stream, that was Keeper Rickets's home, and also the home of his grandson, one of the cleverest boys at Porlock school when I was there, and who, not so long after that, was lying in that churchyard, having lost his life in the Second World War...

Usually Tom and Liz offered us a drink of some sort before the walk back, as everyone going that way had to pass within touching distance of their little cottage door. And often we would be persuaded to stop off at Silcombe, if it was an afternoon service, and there would be given a wonderful and welcome tea by my Aunt Annie.

From left: David, Tom, Molly, Josie and Margaret in 1934.

Granny Ridd in 1934.

Louie in 1935.

Josie, Tom and Cousin Dick Gregory, circa 1937.

WALKING THROUGH
CULBONE WOODS

The sun filters its dappled antique light
through stunted oaks upon my path.

High up, buzzards call,
soft screaming, plaintive, or hunting so low I hear the rush
of their wings above the trees.

In combes small streams hid
and show, as they slip-trickle
new water over old stone
down to the beach.

Here is eternity in moss and lichen
ancient trees and timeless sounds,
of tides ceaselessly crashing among the rocks,
of winds sighing through the trees, and, silent
but for the bent sedges whisper,
deer move in a straggling group
along the path above.

By a small gully I catch the whiff of fox
newly passed and see in my mind its slinking
obsequious, hunting crawl.

Coming out of the woods,
I strain to keep the essence.
It dies too soon
leaving me lonely and haunted.

PORLOCK SCHOOL

I WAS nearly seven and already able to read and write when we started school at Porlock. Jack went to Brendon and there was no more running off to follow the hounds. We fell in line after a fashion, but were on the wild side compared with the village children.

With more discipline, more teachers and more subjects to be studied, we did well. But it was not quite as simple as that, because we were all pretty mixed-up and often very tired.

I remember one morning at assembly Margaret having the misfortune to yawn just as the very unpopular headmaster was passing. He stood in front of her and did a mimic yawn full in her face. Instantly she lashed out and smacked him across his cheek. There was a hush in the classroom. I longed to applaud, but did not dare.

I could not take in anything of geography or history, with all its wars. The war I was worried about was the one at home.

Mind you, the attendance officer must have been pleased with us! My mother kept us away from home as much as possible, hoping to hide from us the true state of her disastrous marriage.

Never underestimate what a child, especially a nervous child such as I was, half understands and worries about. Knowing so much and being told so little was not at all helpful.

The journey to Porlock School by car was an opportunity, my parents soon realised, for us to bring back various things from the village. Sometimes in the dinner hour we would go for cigarettes for my mother. She smoked Piccadillys, which came in a pretty blue oval tin. How she would keep reminding us of our errand and I can still remember vividly her anguished face when we blithely announced that we had forgotten them. The nearest shop was six miles away and we had no car.

Another thing we would bring back in the school car was the accumulator, which we collected from the hardware store, having left it there a few days earlier to be recharged. This was a large battery, which stored power to run a wireless. It was important, so the shopkeeper impressed upon us, that we keep the battery upright, as any spilled acid would burn our clothes, our skin and the car seats. Visions of evenings without the wireless filled us with as much despair as modern children might feel at the loss of their television.

The school car would also collect two children from Lillycombe, David and Barbara, whose parents had a cottage there. We all got on very well, to the extent that mischief often lurked around us. After school we played a lot in the plantation at the top of the road, usually building little moss houses. Once my brother David accidentally set fire to an old shed in the wood and there was a great fuss. Another time, we persuaded David and Barbara to truant with us: we had done it before and come to no great harm. My brother David has no recollection of playing truant and that figures: it would be more in character for Tom to have led us astray.

I can imagine that the parents of David and Barbara were pretty fed up with us. Twice their father, an ex-policeman, visited our father. He was so tall that his head almost hit the low beams in our house. Pressure was put on my parents to use the strap: that was what he did and he strongly advised my father to do likewise. I am pleased to say my father never did.

What did we learn at Porlock School? I really don't know. I do remember some of the games we played. This one entailed a "shepherd" standing between two lines of children – the sheep and the wolves – calling his sheep.

Shepherd: "Sheep, sheep, come home!"
Sheep: "Can't."
"Why not?"
"Afraid"
"What of?"
"Wolf."
"Wolf's gone to Devonshire,
won't be home for seven year.
Sheep, sheep, come home!"

Whereupon the flock of sheep at one end of the playground would rush towards the pack of wolves at the opposite end and all hell would break lose until someone in authority came to split us up.

Another game I recall had lovely words: "There's fire on the mountains, run, run, run!... Storms on the sea, cat's in the corner and can't catch me..."

It was a good school and in a wild and woolly way I enjoyed it: I liked its size, most of its teachers and the other pupils. But at no time did I get it into my silly head that I should take the whole business of learning more seriously.

David, Margaret and Sheila were the clever ones, who should have had a longer education. Tom and Josie only ever wanted to be on a farm and because it was assumed by our parents that that was our destiny, there seemed little point in stretching our minds for other careers. Exmoor and farming were imprinted all the way through us. And for lazy people – well, it suited me just fine to let others make decisions for me.

Perhaps, had we stayed longer at school, it would have been different. David, Tom and Margaret did go as boarders to Huish and Weirfield schools in Taunton for a very short time, but then the money ran out.

I know Josie and Sheila were pretty upset at the unfairness of it, but I was not at all disappointed. However, I did have to go to another school for a short time. My widowed aunt Ilott, who was suffering from Parkinson's Disease, had now moved from Taunton to Blue Anchor and I stayed with her for a while. Much against my will, I had to attend a small school in Minehead, called Llanberis, where the council offices now are in Blenheim road. Every day I would board the lovely little steam train, now such a tourist attraction, for the short but delightful trip between Blue Anchor and Minehead. But such was my frame of mind that I considered the whole exercise a complete waste of time and money, and it wasn't long before I was truanting again and sent back to Broomstreet.

However, I loved being with my aunt. We did that most magical thing: we made each other laugh, and that was something we both needed. She liked me laughing when I mimicked her movements, especially when it came to helping with things like folding sheets when a certain amount of shaking helped in the process of getting out the creases.

She liked that I enjoyed her food and her long companionable silences and the way she would muse aloud, as if I wasn't there. I remember her saying, relating only to the fact that the news was on the radio, "I wonder how they manage with their rations up at the BBC." For some reason this made me howl with laughter. There were many times when we both laughed so much that tears ran down our cheeks.

"The Pet".
©Alfred Vowles

1920s Open air service,
Culbone Church.
©Alfred Vowles

1920s Meet at Cloutsham. ©Alfred Vowles.

THE BRIGHT LIGHTS

THERE WAS one bus a day into Minehead, which stopped at the top of our lane at around eleven o'clock and departed again from Minehead at quarter past four. This left, after my window gazing, quite a bit of time to use up, which was when I discovered the delights of the cinema. Some of the early films I watched were silent Charlie Chaplins. That's how long ago it was.

I became an avid film fan. The lives of the stars seemed so alluring and so remote from the world I inhabited, that I soon became hooked and found it impossible to leave before the end of the programme.

The snag to this was that the matinee started at two thirty and finished long after the bus back to Broomstreet had gone. I remember the bus driver with great affection: if he could have delayed the bus for half an hour he would have done so.

So, when I entered the cinema I would search the auditorium for any face from "up over" as Exmoor was called by the more civilised people in the town, ever hopeful of seeing someone I knew to give me a lift home. I seldom did.

This meant catching the later bus to Porlock Weir and the long, scary walk up through the woods, in the dark. I soon learned to take a torch in case I was weak enough to give in to my film addiction, and of course like all true addicts I inevitably succumbed. However, I believed that to shine my torch would give away my position, so it was kept for the direst emergencies. That way I felt more in charge of things and I was aware, too, that the batteries would not last long.

My path took me near Ashley Combe Lodge and the tunnels built by the first Lord Lovelace, so that his wife Ada – Lord Byron's daughter – should not have to see the comings and goings of tradesmen and estate workers.

The nightmare of those dark, dank tunnels! Those woods at night were never silent. Stopping from time to time to listen to various rustlings, footfalls real or imagined, of woodland life restless in its sleep, or with perhaps the odd badger snuffling and chuffling along.

I wonder if there are still glow worms in Culbone woods. The first time I saw them I had switched off my torch and was just standing, trying to get my bearings in the dark, having discovered that it was easier to feel my way by looking up to where an outline of trees on either side of the path was faintly etched against the sky. On looking down again, I saw several little greenish lights, and this was my introduction to the magical little glow worms. Yet, by torchlight they turned out to be disappointingly black and dreary-looking, elongated beetles...

Then the fear of awakening the vengeful spirits of all my dead ancestors, as I passed, unworthy lightweight, on the path below Culbone Church!

Leaving that terrifying bit of the journey behind, I could relax and breathe again, but only just. It would be another two miles before I got to six gates, a hundred yards from home, and then all the bottled tension would go and I'd run back like the clappers and fall into bed thinking now only of the film. And wondering...

When I think back now to the absolute fear that accompanied me on those occasions, I wonder at my courage.

Nevertheless, I had no intention of giving up my addiction. The fixes were not too frequent, perhaps every six weeks or so. In the end, it was my father who suggested that I ride to Porlock Weir, stable my horse at the pub, and pick it up after the cinema.

I thought this even worse than going on foot, pointing out that in the dark the pair of us, horse and I, would go over the cliff edge and land on the beach. My father assured me that horses could see better in the dark than humans and insisted that the journey would be safer and much quicker on horseback. Deciding that this was something he might just be right about, I tried out his suggestion – and he was right.

Horse and I, with growing confidence, sometimes galloped most of the way home in the dark.

BROOMSTREET COMBE

I UNDERSTAND the following poem was already at the farm when my parents moved in in 1921. I have included it here because it is so good and of its time, and written long before our lane was tarmacked and, more importantly, long before the small pine plantation was destroyed.

I love the first line reminding me of the cart track winding through the pines and the fun we had in those woods.

> The cart track winds amid the pines
> six miles from Porlock town,
> Thro' purple heather, ribbon fern
> and bracken tinged with brown.
>
> The track anon becomes a lane
> where wild flowers make a sheen
> and stone built walls are carpeted
> with moss in shades of green.
>
> Seen thro' the hills, the sea, the sea!
> Then follows down and down,
> Drink deep long draughts of salted air
> six miles from Porlock town.
>
> Then by the woods of larch and fir
> of beech and mountain ash.
> Here strawberries wild and raspberries
> and there a water splash.
>
> A crystal stream in torrent falls
> O'er moss grown rocks adown
> and threads its path thro' Broomstreet combe
> six miles from Porlock town.

The signature is not clear but looks like E. S. Keate.

The lane from the A39 Porlock to Lynmouth road ran down to the farm through a small fir plantation. It was full of dark, scary recesses, where occasional puffs of smoke in the winter might betray a crouching, shabby. overcoated tramp, poking sticks into a fire. As schoolchildren, together, we might go and talk to him. Alone, it was a different story. I would pass very slowly, holding my breath, trying to look normal and unconcerned, as I believed that tramps, like dogs, must never see that you are afraid, and only when I got out into the light did I dare look back.

In these woods we built shelters with fir branches, made dense and almost waterproof with great clods of moss.

We played truant from here, watching from a dark distance as the school car come and waited. We thought the driver would never move off, but eventually he turned his car round and drove back to Porlock without us.

The problem then was not being able to gauge the time. Tom had no pocket watch and we girls no wrist watches. We built a lovely new house of greenery and I think we must have eaten our school lunch far too early, for time began to hang heavy and we began to feel decidedly peckish. After much argument, fearing the consequences, we broke rank, and the wimps amongst us went sheepishly home at least two hours before we should have – and the game was up.

I remember with great sadness the sea of destruction during the war, when all the trees were felled. We were exposed: all was sky and light. Our trees lay naked in high piles, straight and all the same length, amidst the brushwood. Then they were taken away to be used in an even darker place, as pit props down a coalmine.

THE LIKENESS TAKER

I REMEMBER so well that hectic morning.

My mother and Louie were frantically trying to get us ready to catch the bus to Minehead, which entailed an uphill walk of a mile before we even reached the bus stop. We children, mulish, uncooperative and very resentful, were wanting to stay at home to climb trees and ride horses, hating being dressed up and the sudden critical interest in our appearance.

Louie's voice, harsh and urgent, kept calling, "Watch the clock ... watch the clock," as if it too would join in this deranged scheme to get us all immortalised on a photograph.

Margaret sniffed and scowled as my mother tried to strangle her fine hair into a plait. Several cats wound themselves around our ankles. "Will... you... get... out," my mother said to them from time to time.

Tom shouted to all or any of us whose duty he deemed it to be, "Why don't somebody feed these damn cats?"

Grannie, passing through, holding a newborn lamb, dropped it on the kitchen floor. "Who said that?" she demanded.

Nobody answered, but she knew, so she hauled Tom over to the kitchen sink to wash out the damn with nasty green soap, and Tom, of course, made a great fuss and gagged all about the room.

Josie wailed from upstairs, "I can't find me stockings. Louie, I can't find me stockings."

Louie mumbled, from the side of her mouth not taken up with a safety pin, "Keep looking, I put them out this morning." Then, turning to the rest of us, "Watch the clock ... watch the clock... you must be off in five minutes."

The cats were mewing, the lambs bleating, and Grannie was complaining, "All this fuss just to go to thic ole likeness taker," sounding like the only intelligent being in the house, or so we thought.

Mother, not far from hysteria, said, "Grannie, will you take these animals out." Then, turning to Tom, "Don't let me hear you use that word again... and pull up your socks ... and how on earth have you managed to get your knees so dirty already this morning?"

Tom said, "It's not fair, everybody's always picking on me, and anyway I've lost me garters!"

For reply, Grannie put the lamb down again and gave him a sharp clip on the ear.

Now Louie has started on my hair and with much pulling and tugging secures most of it with a tight red ribbon.

Josie appears wearing odd stockings, one with a big hole in the knee. "Up you go and get the right stockings, or you wont get your photograph taken at all."

"I don't want to be in a silly old photograph anyway, so there."

David, Margaret and Sheila are as ready as they will ever be, all looking sullen and muttering that they don't see why they should be made all silly and smart just for a stupid old photographer.

Then they are told what they had been secretly dreading. "You lot go on ahead and tell the driver that your mother's coming."

They are appalled and gasp with the embarrassment of it.

I thought that I should go to the lavatory before such an ordeal and met Grannie on the way. She was decanting ewe's milk into a bottle with a teat on it to feed the orphan lambs.

When I came out and would have rushed past, she called, "Here, not so fast, young lady, you'll soon catch tothers up. Get that other lamb for me."

Making a grab for the lamb sheltering under a shelf of tins and jars of various veterinary substances, I dislodged a tin of bright red marking fluid. Some of it ran down my skirt and ran dripping down my stockings. I started to rub frantically.

"Don't rub it, you silly little dastard, you'll make it worse."

I began to cry and Grannie tried to comfort me. "It don't show... not too much it don't. Anyway, you got time to change."

But we both knew that there was nothing to change into, that is, nothing suitable for a likeness taker's studio.

1938 "The Likeness Taker" From left: Tom, Margaret, Molly, Sheila, David, Josie

EMBELLE WOOD BEACH

AT TIMES of stress, which often included the school holidays, Nurse May came to stay with us.

Outings with Nurse May were mostly to Embelle Wood beach.

This was no bucket and spade beach, like the ones I had read about in storybooks, where children built sandcastles, romped and swam.

Flanked by the steep wooded slope up to the farms above, Embelle Wood Beach was an area of outstanding wildness, strewn with boulders, rocks and pebbles, an area where for some reason you looked over your shoulder from time to time.

In later years, going there alone I would experience times of unease, times of almost fear, especially at high tide, when the sound of the waves ceaselessly crashing over rocks increased the sense of one's own isolation.

But before this, there was Nurse May. She took us down to the beach, where we ate a few sandwiches, lit a small fire, had a bit of a paddle and maybe a careful dip, before making the long, slow, journey home. To my shame, I seem to remember that Tom and I were the two complainers: I do not recall any of the others whining as much as we two could.

Nurse May was there for the years when we were too young to go alone. When she became too old to do the long haul to the beach, she sort of melted out of our lives and went back to Sussex. She did, though, live to be well into her nineties.

After she left, we were in the tender care of David and Tom.

With Louie scrubbing on hands and knees, and so many of us children wanting to go in and out of the house, she or my mother would tell us to go out and play and not to come back until dinner time, usually with the suggestion that we go to the beach. If my father happened to be around and feeling morning-afterish, any such order might be given with the aim of keeping us out of sight and out of mind. His voice could shrivel a child at ten paces.

So going to the beach seemed the least bad option, and with no nurse May to look after us, things became a little more exciting and a little more precarious.

There were times when we came near to being cut off by the tide and the race along the jagged rocks to safety, with the grey sea seeming to reach out for us as we passed.

On one occasion we lost all our footwear. Putting our shoes in a pile well away from the sea, we wandered off, finding such interesting things to do that they were completely forgotten until it was time to go home. I remember the painful walk back on the rough track. I remember too the look on my mother's face when she took in the loss, and the enormity of finding the money for five new lots of footwear.

Sometimes in the fruit season we would take our walks along the beach as far as Glenthorne. Here if we were lucky, and there was no one around, we could walk home the long way, which took us alongside the orchard. No plums or apples ever tasted better and on those occasions we did not return home starving.

I remember being on the beach with Margaret and Josie when we saw a most eerie lifting and falling of something large and white across the beach between the rocks. Because there was no wind, we knew it was not a piece of white cloth waving in the breeze. We edged warily forward and, eventually, we realised that it was a huge and, to us, completely unfamiliar, bird.

Although gannets are quite usual along the high cliffs of small, isolated islands with rocky ledges, we had never seen one on Embelle Wood beach. It allowed us to lift it and measure it, to marvel at its size and great wingspan. It was beautiful, with its large eyes outlined in fine black feathers, its long, black-tipped wings and, most of all, the faintly orange head fading into white towards the clean lines of its beak.

But this was a very sick bird, too weak to scramble through the rocks. We carried it to a level spot but, although bright of eye and quite alert, it made no attempt to escape us, nor did it seem unduly worried at being carried.

Next came a long argument on what we should do. Margaret said we should leave it there and let nature take its course. Josie and I both wanted to take it home.

"It's a *sea* bird," Margaret insisted, "it lives on *fish*," irritating us by the pressure she put on the words sea and fish, all the more so because we knew she was right.

"We've got fish at home," I said.

"That's *tinned* fish," she retorted, growing more and more ratty by the minute, then walking off in a huff.

After we had watched her disappear into the dense, low, scrubby woodland, I took control as the oldest and told Josie that we had the choice of taking the gannet down to the water's edge or taking it home with us and putting it on the pond. "If it gets better," I said, "we could bring it back and put it in the sea." I desperately wanted to take this beautiful bird home with me.

Josie was about seven at the time and I was ten. We both looked doubtfully at the bird, as big as a goose, then cast our eyes further up the steep sides of the wooded cliffs, knowing that it would have to be carried 900 feet up to the farm.

I shall always remember that journey – and so does Josie. We struggled bravely, even making light of the climb, until we had passed the halfway position. After that there was no turning back, no admitting to a very bad mistake.

When we eventually arrived at the farm, we were totally exhausted, but not so exhausted that we were incapable of justifying our actions. No one argued or challenged us, and perhaps there was even a slight admiration in the eyes of our-father-which-art.

We put the wan, sad bird on the pond, hoping to see it at least rejoice a bit by swimming a length, but no, it floated listlessly at the water's edge, refusing all food. I feel sure that, even if we had had a live sardine, it would have refused that too.

After three days and innumerable visits to the pond, we found it dead one morning before school. So ended our love affair with a beautiful gannet.

On that strip of beach called Embelle Wood were many connections with Broomstreet farm, and with my family.

Just off this beach, during the war, an oil tanker was struck by a mine, and here was horror – so far unimagined by me – of the reality of war. From the cliff top we watched the ending of many lives, while helpless aircraft hovered overhead and the sea burned all around the stricken tanker.

Another drama occurred when two ships ran aground in the fog on Embelle Wood beach. The first we knew of it was when police and coastguard vehicles rushed down our lane. Having to pause long enough to open a gate, and asked what were they hurrying for, they told us what had happened.

When Margaret heard this, she took off down the lane, into the woods and straight down the cliff, clutching and falling all the way to the beach. On arrival, she was met by Greek seamen who were unable to make themselves understood. The other ship was Irish and none of their sailors had yet got ashore. Soon the police and coast guards arrived and took over. A few months later, however, Margaret was presented with a huge and splendid box of chocolates for being the first on the scene.

Here on this beach my great-uncle John Red built a boathouse and a house that was never lived in.

I never knew great-uncle John, because he died before I was born, but I learned quite a lot about him from my cousin Dick Gregory.

Apparently he was a very grey man, with a grey face, a grey moustache and grey clothes. He was also a very heavy smoker.

Among his many enterprises, he built limekilns and brought lime and coal from Wales in his own boat called the Eleanor Mary, which was the name my parents chose for me, although I was always known as Molly. The limestone and coal were brought ashore in smaller boats, unloaded on Embelle Wood Beach and hauled up to the kiln.

He had always spent a lot of time on the beach, looking out for what was washed ashore. Broomstreet when my parents moved in was packed in every available space with stuff brought up from the beach, including beams and planks of wood, especially hard woods.

He had been most reluctant to leave Broomstreet after my parents moved in. My mother told me that in the end the only way of getting him out was to take his bed down to Littlewood, where his sister Elizabeth had already set up home.

Great-uncle John, feeling confined and useless, being pensioned off and sent to live in a small cottage, with no farm to run, must have despaired. His visits to Embelle Wood and the beach were now almost a necessity.

It would seem that Lady Lovelace gave great-uncle John permission to build a house on Embelle Wood Beach. Perhaps she had smiled to herself and put the request down to the ramblings of an old man?

At some stage he must have told his sister that he was building a new house for them, and she, old and absent-minded, might not have even heard or taken in what he had said. Indeed, such a foolish thought could surely never be taken seriously? They were both old; provisions would have had to be brought from Porlock Weir or Brendon on horseback. As for great-aunt Elizabeth, she would have had to say goodbye to any visits to or from any friend or relative. There would have been just her grey brother and his eccentric grey ways. An added reason for wanting to stay around Littlewood was that my mother had started to have babies and great-aunt Elizabeth was not going to miss seeing her great-nephews and nieces grow up.

There came a time when the building was getting so far ahead that he thought it time to advise his sister of its progress. The walls of the rooms were up and the house now only required a roof.

Imagine the scene when he began proudly to announce that the cottage was almost ready to move into. Elizabeth must have looked at him as if he had gone mad. Under no circumstances would she move down. "You go!" she must have screamed at him. And perhaps she said, as I might have done: "And the sooner the better."

How he must have worked at his dream and how he must have grieved at its total impossibility without the help of his sister.

I wish I had known him, for it seems odd that such a grey man turned out to be such a fascinating character.

The house would have been very primitive. When we children came to investigate it, quite a few years later, some tall bits of walls were still standing. Several rooms were outlined in the ruins, including a small one, presumably intended to be the lavatory. Over the years sheep and deer wandered in and out of great-uncle John's cottage. At very high tide, it must have been flooded.

His boat shed was also still there, pretty tumbledown, but useful for us in the rain or to eat our sandwiches in...

Here on this beach my cousin accidentally set the hillside burning...

Here on this beach my brother found a decomposing body...

Here, by being so often on this beach, we perhaps saved our parents' sanity...

One of my regrets is that now, with negotiable tracks washed away, I am no longer able to get there.

The Glenthorne Estate Tenantry, circa 1920.
Top row from left: Jim Woollacott, Gabriel Litson, P Ettering (?), B Huxtable (?), John Ridd, William Squire, Charlie Squire
Middle row: G Graham, John Nercombe, G Ash, B Palmer, Mr Stapledon (Estate agent), Mr T Barrow, Mr Squire (Blue Ball), Mr Richards (carpenter). Bottom row: John Coles, Bert Lethaby, George Huxtable, William French, MDN, Clerk to Mr Stapledon.

Sheep shearing at Ash Farm, when the Priscotts were there in the late 1920s From left: Alfie Keal, Bill Kent, Ernest Westcott, Ernest Richards (my father), Jim Land (with beard), Richard Richards (holding barrel), Jack Woollacott, Tom Ridd, Herbert Richards (with pipe), Irvin Red (of Pitt), Tom Priscott, Nath Cook (Parsonage Farm).

LITTLEWOOD

BEFORE THE present farm cottage was built, around 1840, at a cost reputedly in the region of £45, Littlewood was the cottage that went with Broomstreet Farm.

After the death of her husband, great-aunt Elizabeth lived on at Littlewood alone, apart from a year or two when she took in a chap who worked on the farm.

The occupant I remember with most affection was Miss Woollacott, who lived there during the war. She was a sister of Aunt Annie at Silcombe and Aunt Ada at Yearner, so to all our cousins she was Aunt Julie. Such was the fashion of the times that, since she was not our aunt, we had to call her Miss Woollacott, which seemed to me very unfair, as she was such a kind, friendly person, with an air of determined optimism, that you could not help warming to her.

Aunt Julie – I am going to call her that now – was approached one day at the beginning of the war by a man of about fifty. After a long conversation, he persuaded her to let him lodge there for a week or so. Perhaps she would be considered nowadays as rather gullible, but she had spent a lifetime being obliging to her own family of nieces and nephews – as was the fate of most unmarried women then – and I doubt very much if she had ever had dealings with anyone who was not straightforward and honest.

Her lodger was viewed with suspicion by many of us and we decided he must be a spy, for he was forever roaming around in the woods and on the beach.

On one of Aunt Julie's daily visits to the farm for her post, milk and eggs, she confessed that he had been there for two months and, so far, not paid her a single penny. Every week he told her some plausible story about his money coming through quarterly and that it was cast-iron safe. We could see that she wanted to be rid of him.

Shortly after that, he left. Because he had brought no luggage, it was some time before Aunt Julie realised he had gone for good. But while he might have gone away empty-handed – so, too, was Aunt Julie.

I still believe he was a spy. I used to see lights offshore at night and, from Littlewood, hear voices on the beach or out at sea. Occasionally I would find a dry cigarette newly dropped on my Embelle Wood path and have a sense of a presence nearby, although there was no one around.

But then, I always did have too much imagination. And would a spy really run off without paying his bills?

After this experience, she must have been very pleased to take in some of the airmen we all had billeted on us. They all liked her very much and, for her, it must have been a happy time with such cheerful young company, removing some of the hurt she had suffered at the hands of her last, unpaying guest.

In due course, she gave up her tenancy of Littlewood and I came into contact with her again, when she moved in with aunt Ilott at Blue Anchor, in the later stage of the latter's illness.

I think Littlewood must have been empty then for a year or two before it was refurbished and lived in again by Lady Tryon, a relative of the landlord.

THE GAMES WE PLAYED

I HAVE been reminded in the writing of this book of how often people visiting the farm and seeing its isolation and so many of us youngsters around would exclaim, "What on earth do you all do with yourselves here?" I for one could not imagine what could be on offer in a more urban environment. After all, we had the whole of Exmoor to play in.

There was nothing happening anywhere so far as we were concerned that encroached upon our lives. We lived too far from Porlock and Lynton for my brothers even to be considered for a football team. We were not even able to envisage the importance other children attached to birthdays. Christmas was different and we had plenty of presents and parties then. But in my family, no one ever celebrated birthdays beyond saying, rather grudgingly, Happy birthday to whoever had one on that day, and birthday presents were virtually unheard of.

We created our own entertainment. David was our ideas man, presumably because, being the oldest, he was told to keep us smaller ones occupied. I do recall that most activities he devised for us, he never actually took part in himself.

Once he made a cemented, box-shaped hidey-hole in a field, where we could each put in one thing we thought precious. He showed us how to lift a heavy flat stone over it so that no one would ever know it was there. I was very curious as to what Margaret had put in the sealed packet she left there. But she was stubborn, so I never knew.

What I put in was my blue Jesus book. I desperately wanted Jesus to stop my old aunt from teasing me that I loved my cousin Henry, because I most certainly did not. This was the same aunt who could not believe that anyone in the world could not like trifle. I had been taught to eat what I was given and always say thank you, which meant that she kept refilling my plate as fast as I forced it down. To make matters worse, she did this with a merry chuckle and I was convinced that she knew and was doing it to be beastly.

The blue Jesus book came out the following week and for me that was God's last chance.

There was a game we called Keep the Kettle Boiling, which meant climbing up a vertical ladder, taking a running jump over a ten foot drop, on to the small window shaped hole on the opposite wall, leaping to the ground, running around the building, up the ladder and around again. The thing was not to baulk at the leap and not to hesitate. Easy enough for those of ten or twelve, but terrifying for me, and doubly so for Josie at five.

As we grew older more exciting games were thought of, and to this day, the one I remember with most satisfaction was boulder rolling.

We came upon this diversion by accident. Coming home from the beach one day, in a hurry to get back for some reason or other, we left the long, meandering path in favour of walking straight up the side of the hill.

Scrambling through undergrowth, pulling ourselves up by any available means, we came upon a large teetering rock, which we managed to send down to the beach. This proved to be such a dramatic, destructive, leaping journey, before it touched bottom and hit the rocks below, that we immediately tried to do it again – but without success.

David and Tom pondered this for a while and then found the answer in leverage and bar irons (or to those of you who don't come from Exmoor – iron bars).

We would wait for a day when we saw our parents go away. David and Tom would collect bar irons and off we would go the to last field above the woods, climb the hedge, work our way along the boundary keeping mostly, but not always, to the Glenthorne side. While Margaret, Josie and I set to work, each collecting a pile of big stones, David and Tom spent a considerable amount of time selecting the largest most suitable boulder, that was not too firmly embedded in the soil and did not possess any sharp angles, which might cause it to come to a stop before gathering up enough speed to start its hectic leaping journey nine hundred feet down to the beach below.

We let the boys get their bar irons underneath the boulder, before we moved forward. It was all action then, we girls in position, lying on our backs, six, small, booted feet flat against the boulder. After a fair amount of practice, we knew without a word being spoken exactly when to put some of our store of stones underneath.

How to describe the excitement of those teetering moments? With one last almighty leverage and push the thing toppled over, and, slowly at first, the great giant of a boulder, launched, I felt, like a threat to the world, began to gather speed. At each small tree that snapped, at each other boulder that might be in its path and jumped over, we were breathless with our daring. Too soon, it was heard to crash on to the beach below.

There were "what if?" moments, put forward by David, which were quickly dismissed. These were remote woods and that was a remote and deserted beach below. How likely was it that anyone would be hurt? Compared to the pleasure we had, we decided it was well worth the risk.

All good things come to an end. I don't know how long it took to the day of serious adult faces confronting us. There had been complaints, hadn't we thought of the consequences of our actions? People walking the beach had been terrified. People walking the path below had nearly been crushed.

At a loose end again, David decided to make us a seesaw. He was not one to do things in a small way. The seesaw was good. It was the siting of it that had not been given serious thought. Really there were few suitable flat places that would also be out of sight of the house, and that was important to us all.

Anyone falling off, it was very high, would go rolling down the steep, possibly breaking their neck – at least that was what my father said when he saw it.

We had many happy times on it, until the day, with our parents away, and with Josie and Margaret on one side and Sheila, the youngest, on the other, and me, not on the thing, just taking care by holding the end of the plank that it didn't go too high, when for some reason I let go. I don't know if I slipped or what, but the result was that up Sheila went and off she came.

Obviously in great pain, she screamed at us that she had broken her neck. This is where I would like to say that we ran to comfort and reassure her. Not a bit of it. Fear beating compassion, we hurried her indoors, got her to bed and told her not to make a sound when our parents came home.

When they came back, not much later, they seemed to be in a fairly amiable mood, asking what we had done all day, the usual stuff. It might have been a quarter of an hour before my mother smelt a rat, and all that time we were keeping an anxious ear for any sounds from above. All was quiet until our mother asked, "Where is Sheila?" whereupon that same Sheila, who had been listening in her bedroom above, let out an almighty scream.

Someone was sent on horseback for the doctor, who arrived in due course and pronounced another broken collarbone, I think the fourth.

After that, we soon settled back into routine. Sheila was going to live, and I was not a murderer.

Of all the dangerous games we thought up, I suppose the one involving an old silk bedspread was the most alarming. On blowy days, we had frequently tried to take off from the top field with a parachute made from a sheet, but with little success. The clever ones amongst us declared that the problems were caused by lack of wind and the material of the sheet not being finely woven enough. *Everyone* knew that parachutes were made of *silk*.

The day came when the conditions were just right. There was a howling gale, quite the windiest we had had since the idea of taking off had come to us, and we had a much better parachute.

I remember it was getting dark, so we had to hurry. By a circuitous route we ran around the buildings, hoping no one would ask where we were going and what we were carrying, which was the silk bedspread.

And it was a success! All of us had a go, never one at a time, for we realised that would be too risky, and occasionally we had to use the shelter of the hedge to slow the parachute down.

I don't know which of us thought of sending Josie up, "Just to see how far she would go."

We positioned ourselves to catch the greatest gust of the wind in which we were having difficulty in keeping our feet on the ground, cajoled Josie into hanging on, and, at a given signal, all let go.

Too late now to instruct her to let go. Anyway she could not have heard in the gale. In the twinkling of an eye she was airborne, flying up and away. First she reached a high hedge and we were each of us praying that this would stop her. But no, over the top she went and to our horror we realised she was heading towards the sea.

We ran like the dickens to the other side of the hedge, where there was no sign of her. Then, to our immense relief, we saw her furious face come crawling up the hill!

Amongst the many other things we were told not to do, and did when no one was around, was baiting the bull. I do not remember David or Tom being in on this, so perhaps they were at school or at work.

When Charlie had let the bull out to drink in the yard, making sure that all gates were shut, he would go off to do an hour's work before putting the bull back into its house. Presumably making believe that we were matadors, we would go to the bottom step of the open flight of stairs up into the barn and wave whatever we had to hand. If this didn't get the desired effect, we'd venture into the yard. Then, as the bull lowered his head and started to charge, we would rush up the steps as fast as we could, falling over each other and flushed with pride at our adventure. I tremble to think of what would have happened had any of us slipped.

When we were small, our father was quite inventive in teaching us how not to drown. Knowing how attracted we were to playing in or by the pond, we were told that sometimes a bogey man visited the ponds and hid in the bushes for children playing where they had been told not to.

Half afraid and half disbelieving, we tested the boundaries from time to time, getting nearer and braver, finally dancing along the narrow bank that ran beside the pond. We skimmed stones, measured its depth with a long pole, and waded in its murky waters up to chest height, daring each other to go in deeper. All was well.

Then, one day there was the most horrendous growl, followed by a deep booming roar, and we were off, running home, bootless, shoeless and terrified.

So it became time to teach us to swim. This was done by the age-old method of throwing us in one at a time, whilst my father, fully clothed, issued orders from the bank above. He had with him a long pole, which we were to grab if in real difficulties. How many mouthfuls of that foul water did we swallow before he figured that it was safe to leave us alone in the pond?

Hunting for us was out of the question, not having the right clothes or the right horses. My mother, from whom we mostly took our lead, was aware that realistically it could not be done. Hunting is and was a very expensive sport. With a different husband, in different circumstances, she would have been a very keen follower. Our cousins at Silcombe and Yearnor and many of our school friends all enjoyed going out with the local hunts.

Shooting was a different matter. At the farm we had two twelve bore double-barrelled guns. We persuaded our-father-which-art to let us, that is Josie and myself, take them out rabbiting. After long lectures on safety catches, not going to the same field together lest we shoot each other, and suchlike, we set off. Together!

I suppose Josie would have been around thirteen years old, and me sixteen. All was well until the day when climbing a stile behind Josie, I wrenched my ankle as I jumped down on the other side. Immediately there was a loud explosion and a large dark shape flew through the air and landed at her feet.

"You got that one Molly," she said in great excitement.

We both looked at the ground and right next to her foot was a large hole where I'd shot the ground from (almost) under her feet. Luckily she still had all her toes.

Our mistake was in telling this story – which we thought highly amusing – at home. It ended up with us being actively discouraged, I won't say forbidden – the forbidding days were almost over – from shooting. We gave up largely because we both disliked administering the final chop when anything was not killed outright.

My leanings towards pyrotechnics perhaps started with the making of little fires with matches and a few twigs, out of sight and well away from those who would most certainly say no. I used to long to have my own flaming torch so that I could go out in the fields and set light to the numerous fuzz (furze) bushes in various fields on the farm. One day, catching my father in a rather jolly mood, I asked for and got my own way and was supplied with a long piece of copper piping stuffed with old stockings, all heavily impregnated with paraffin. He would not give me the matches but lit it for me and sent me hurrying along the lane to do my damnedest.

Touching the flame to the dry, brown, under-part of any fuzz bush I selected, feeling the heat, seeing the flames and sparks, hearing all the snap and crackle was true bliss and truly exciting.

It lingers, that wanting of a conflagration, though milder, now that I have discovered fear of fire. Just a few years ago, or so it seems – it was in fact thirty-five years or more, when my husband John was alive and we were living at Littlewood – looking out of the window across a great stretch of woodland, he remarked on a patch of furze growing there. Knowing of my tendencies, he suggested that my friend Margrit and I went over and put a match to it. It was nearly dark, so I knew that it would be dramatic. We set off for our walk and nervously started to burn the bushes, aware that there was an audience of John and three children watching from the far off window.

I wonder to this day what made John suggest such a foolhardy venture.

Almost dark now, we watched, with nervous pleasure, the furze burn, when suddenly flames leapt up a nearby fir tree, played around the top, moved to the next and the next, until I thought the whole woods would be aflame. In a panic I began to run.

"Where are you going?" Margrit shouted after me.

"To get John," I shouted back.

"What good is a man at a time like this?" she called back to me.

Indeed!

What we saw that night, when flames leapt from tree to tree, leaving not one of them with as much as a scorch mark, was dramatic all right. Someone suggested that it must have been atmospheric and something to do with resins exuded by the fir trees caused by the heat from the burning furze bushes.

The Gathering of the Exmoor Ponies ©Alfred Vowles.

Mr Robert Westcott's Luncheon Party at Alderman's Barrow ©Alfred Vowles.

1920s Blackmore Gate monthly auction ©Alfred Vowles.

SOME OF THE PRACTICALITIES

DELIVERIES TO the farm, before the lane was made up, were unknown, because tradesmen refused to come down. So we put a large galvanised container adjacent to the road for their use.

For a household of eleven or twelve sitting down to eat three times a day, a lot of provisions were called for. In the tin box, as we called it, would be left, meat, fish, fruit and groceries, hardware and mountains of bread. My mother made lots of our bread but there were just so many of us.

The tin box was big enough to take one or two small children. Whilst waiting for the school car, in the rain, it was sometimes used for that, until the time I had earwigs down my neck.

One foggy morning I was up at the top of the lane, by the box with my father, when we heard a stag roaring close by, but could see nothing except thick mist. My father roared back and after a pause we could hear it getting nearer. When it roared again, I was rather frightened, especially when my father tucked me under his fawn raincoat, put his hands in the air to look like antlers, and roared again.

Now it was close by and we could see it, puzzled at whatever was roaring so realistically. It came closer, raising its head and roaring again, and I fled for the safety of the tin box. My father, a bit worried himself now, stopped his play-acting and started shouting at the stag, with much undignified jumping about and waving of arms.

The stag, annoyed, stood his ground, dropped his head, lifted it again, snorted, and then, in its own good time, turned and walked majestically away.

Transport was always a problem, so that people who came from quite short distances often overnighted.

There was a Mrs Arnold who came up from Porlock to make chair covers and curtains and stayed until the job was done. All that material strewn about the place. All the bits tacked together from the inside, the careful turning of it, and finally pristine chintz covers, transforming our shabby rooms.

The farrier too came and often had to stay overnight, because he lived at Exford. There was an occasion when he saved Tom's life. It was just after Christmas and all of us were at the table when Tom went blue in the face, unable to breathe. While my mother stood half way to the table, carrying a large treacle pudding, Farrier Adams picked Tom up, dangled him by his feet, and then gave him a tremendous thump between the shoulder blades. Out came the small but sharp strip of metal from a cheap whistle he had had from a Christmas cracker and had been persistently blowing, much to everyone's irritation.

Often at dinnertime Nath Cook would call in if he was doing work around our lanes, keeping the hedges trimmed and the gutters clear. He lived at Culbone Parsonage and worked for the council. He must have been the most inoffensive, quiet man I ever heard speak. It was not that he wasn't interesting: he had lived in the area all his life and was laden with stories of local people and their pasts. He took his place on the window seat of the farm kitchen, was given a cup of tea, took out his sandwiches, and began.

Almost at once I was overcome with drowsiness and half an hour later would look around at us all and be amazed that we were not all asleep. It would be with an effort that I could raise myself to eat my pudding.

It was a happy day when the lane was at last tarmacked. Vans delivered bread from Stenners; fruit, vegetables and fish from Westcotts; and groceries from Clapps of Lynton. Then there was the dark blue van that so scared me when I first saw it. Emblazoned along its side were the words, which even now I consider a bit of a non sequitur – Family Butcher. My father was *very* scary!

So it was the end of the tin box.

However, before it went, one amusing incident came about when the paying guests (we called them visitors) asked Louie where the meet was that day. She, thinking catering and meat, said, "It will be up in the tin box this morning." They hastily walked away convinced, as Louie said, that she was simple.

And yet there was a small disappointment, now the school car was able to use the lane. I had hated the walks to school at Oare, and to the church, but never to the same degree that walk up the lane. I loved it where the walls ran along the bottom part of the lane. There we could find birds' nests, wonderful lichens and mosses, violets, primroses, ragged robin, cow parsley and wood sorrel. It was the secret green things that most attracted me, especially, for some reason, the pennywort, not pretty, but pushing its way through every break in the stonework. Sometimes I would just go off on my own, walking along Yenworthy lane peering into the magic of eye level walls.

The heavy and large equipment needed then for a washing day took up so much space; it was lucky that we had plenty.

A boiler stood in one corner, a fixture. Each Monday my mother would get up at six to light the little fire under it. There was such a lot of washing, with six children and four adults all the time, and if it was summer time there would be all the bed linen from the people staying in the house for their holidays. The nightmare of winter was all the woollens, all that drying...

There would be a large tub of blue, another of starch, and another for soaking. The very big and heavy wooden mangle had to be wheeled into position. My mother smoked more cigarettes on a Monday than on any other day of the week. By breakfast, prepared by Louie, she would have smoked far too many. The tarmacked drive meant that we were, eventually, able to have our laundry collected.

The first cooking stove I remember was one with an open fire on the top. This was kept going night and day with tree trunks and very big logs. Letting it go out would have meant a late breakfast. The kettle hung from a crook, as did cauldrons. Underneath, there was the oven, underneath the oven, a long wide shallow tray of hot ashes.

Out of this wonderful arrangement would come the most delicious crusty bread. It was a deep oven and entailed getting down on the kitchen floor, on hands and knees, and with a long wooden spatula thing retrieving the bread from the back.

Good old-fashioned roasts and Yorkshire puddings would be fished out, and fruit cakes and sponges. How my mother managed to get so many different foods requiring different temperatures, out of the same simple oven is astonishing.

The next stove was a Cook and Heat, a black-leaded stove with brass handles and knobs. This was beautiful to look at, created some hot water, but was not up to the job for such a large household. Next she tried a bottled gas stove. That lasted no more than a couple of years, and lastly, the Aga, for us it was the best, the most suitable and labour saving of the lot. It was though a coke stove. This created so much dust when being filled that in the end it was taken out and an oil fired Aga put in. At last a stove my mother was happy with.

Later on, after Louie had left, I was in charge of the visitors. I enjoyed this, for I liked seeing new faces and meeting new people. Actually, many of our visitors came back again and again, though, I must admit, not as many as came back for Louie's tender care. And we made some good friends. We often had music and singsongs, a few guests bringing their own instruments. My father would join in, for above all he loved a bit of jollity and indeed would have liked a life with no responsibility at all.

There was one occasion when I went to prepare the evening meal and found the chicken decidedly whiffy. There were no refrigerators then, though we did have a cool salting house. The weather must have been very muggy for a day or two, for even though I washed the bird with salt and vinegar and gave it a strong thyme stuffing there was still a gamy smell.

I threatened to go on strike. Nothing, I said, would induce me to take stinking chicken in to people expecting a good wholesome dinner after a day of walking on Exmoor. But there was nothing else prepared.

In the end I had to play my part. The meal was delivered to them and very soon their bell rang. Full of foreboding I went in, only to be asked for more gravy. As I was leaving the room, this hard northern male voice said, "What's the game?" which I took in the what-are-you-playing-at sense. "What's the game?" he repeated. "I bet my missus it was pheasant."

Collecting my few wits I told him he was wrong. "Actually, it's grouse," I said.

*Haymaking
picnic, 1942
From left: Taffy
(an airman),
Margery from
Broomstreet
Cottage, my
mother, my father,
Tom, another
airman, Margaret
At front : Josie,
Sheila.*

*1942 David
cultivating.*

*1942 At Oare
Village Hall.*

BOTTLES AND JARS

ONE OF the great pleasures of country living then was the sight and the taste of rows and rows of home made pickles, jams and marmalade, of bottles of fruit and of the black laver.

Laver meant another Embelle Wood adventure among the rocks where it grew, if we were lucky, in thick streamers of seaweed, to be collected as the tide went out. Each of us would have a porous bag of some sort, so that the seawater dripped through, enabling us to carry it home without being weighed down with too much water.

What a performance cooking the stuff! First it had to be washed in several waters so that any green could be picked out and any bits of limpet or gravel removed. It was then put into very large saucepans with around half a pound of butter to each container, a little salt, a cupful of vinegar and twice as much water. Then it must be simmered for hours, with interruptions all the time of, "Is it ready yet?" just as a child keeps asking during a journey, "Are we there yet?" Such was our real longing to have some.

The laver, or laverbread as the Welsh call it, had a very distinctive smell during the cooking, which always made my mouth water, but sent the uninitiated reeling out of the house holding their noses.

There was no fresh fruit in our house – or in most others – except when it was in season, apart from Christmas oranges and Margaret's diet bananas. Margaret was put on bananas because she was thin and pale, though how bananas could make any one less pale I have never discovered.

Apples were stored in one of the rooms, no one fruit touching another. The only ones we were allowed to eat were those that were already showing a spot of rot or shrivelled at the end of the keeping season. Now I watch children in despair as they refuse any fruit not perfect, and I feel how privileged and spoilt they are.

Pears were bottled, plums likewise or made into jam and then there was the ubiquitous gooseberry, never a favourite of mine. It turned up in jams, bottles, pies, pickles, and in fools, and I did not like any of them.

I had similar feelings about beetroot, except when it was young and fresh in the spring.

I cannot finish this list of fruits without mentioning the whortleberry. We did not at all like picking these tiny fruit. Sometimes we did it with an adult, Louie perhaps, and then with much encouragement we managed to bring home a respectable amount. What we dreaded was the use our father made of this as a punishment – just for being children I presume. He would give us impossibly large containers and warn us not to come home until they were filled. I suppose the older members of the family could not have taken this as seriously as I did, believing every threat.

Fridges and freezers are a blessing and a boon to country living, but nothing can match those gleaming, jewel-like colours of a pantry full of bottled fruits.

THE DAIRY

THERE IS now an area of Broomstreet farmhouse that we have allowed to fall into disrepair, no longer able to fight the damp that creeps in from the bank it abuts. I call them the green rooms now, but they used to be my favourite part of the house. Each had an appropriate name. The tap house was presumably so called because it was the first room to have a tap in it. The salting house was where the meat was cured in the slate salter which is still there and where meat hooks still hang from the ceiling.

Then there was the dairy, so cool and fresh. I loved those rooms, smelling of whitewash, and all around the room grey slate shelves with pans of milk, some already scalded with the crusty cream on top or those pans waiting for the cream to rise. I loved the contrast of the brick floors, grey shelves and white walls, so soft a combination of colours.

Devonshire cream is, to my mind, the best. There is though, a lot of waste, unless you have an army of pigs to drink the excess, still rich, milk.

This was where the Aga came into its own for people in the country without electricity. It was so easy to slip the milk pans from the hottest to the cooler hotplate before carting them off to the cool dairy for the cream to rise.

My mother instructed us in all things that any reasonably useful farmer's wife should be able to do. How much notice I took of most of it is debatable. None of us girls ever managed to kill a chicken, as our mother, for all her gentleness, did without a qualm.

But I did enjoy and take seriously the butter making. I liked the ritual. The scalding of the butter prints and the cooling under cold running water, and similar treating of the hands, with water as hot as bearable, then the cold tap until you could no longer stand it. Sometimes, in hot weather, the stirring of the cream took so long that you thought it would never fracture and separate, and at the first imagined sign you would be tempted to add the water too soon, ending up with a greasy watery mess. On a good day, when the butter came quickly and the first lot of butter milk had been taken off, the washing of the butter took place. It had to be washed until it was clear, without a trace of cream to be seen, and then began the noisy, satisfying, butter printing. This was not done just to make the end product more attractive – which it did – but principally to slap all the moisture out, for unless this was done the butter did not keep.

Came the day when our-father-which-art announced the purchase of a second hand separator.

The beauty of the separator was that any waste would be of such poor blue milk, that throwing any away would not be so drastic. We found a use for most of it, some to the pigs, some in poultry mash, and some, believe it or not, was mopped over the red tiled floor after it had been washed. It was as good as any floor polish.

A plus for the women of the household was that the separator meant that there was only one lot of cream to scald. The result, though, was Cornish cream, which was not as crusty as the Devonshire.

Using the separator was heavy work to begin with, turning the handle, stiff and hard (I hear my brother David talking of centrifugal force, somewhere at the back of my mind), it soon became easier, and quite pleasant watching the blue milk coming out of one spout and the cream out of another.

There was one person who very much disapproved of this new contraption, and she was Grannie Richards. Any excuse she could find to interrupt proceedings she would. In the end, and in despair at us being too involved to listen, angry and red in the face with fury, she would say that the farm was going to rack and ruin and all we could do was to bide indoors grinding the milk.

ILLNESSES AND ACCIDENTS

THE FOOD we ate as children was as good and balanced a diet as anyone could wish for. There were always fresh green vegetables, as well as all the fruit, fresh or bottled. We had eggs, home grown bacon, plenty of meat and good homemade bread.

We were also given fish several times a week in one form or another, including cod, which was then a cheap meal and often kippers or bloaters for breakfast. However, the fish we most looked forward to were fresh herrings from Porlock Weir or Minehead.

Despite all this good food, we were also given a daily tablespoonful of cod liver oil and malt.

However, for such a healthy group of children as we seemed to be, we had some real and several imaginary illnesses.

When I was six weeks old, everyone in the household went down with the measles. It was serious enough for Nurse May to have to wean me on to the bottle and for the family at Lillycombe to send down one of their men to do the necessary work outside with the stock. My mother's sister Helen came to stay to lend a hand. She went back a week later with the measles. After this and my rude and early weaning, I became cross-eyed, which was good meat for Tom later on! Fortunately, my affliction went away of its own accord when I was about ten years old.

I must have been about ten, when I thought myself into appendicitis. Yes, there was a small pain in my right side, which came and went, and each time my poor parents had to take me to see Dr. Head who was based in Brendon.

In retrospect I feel sure that it was some sort of cry for attention.

Before Dr Head retired and we were passed on to a doctor in Porlock, he told us that I had a grumbling appendix, that nothing might come of it and that there was nothing to worry about. In the end, the new doctor had me taken to hospital and I had the operation. I really do believe that I manipulated that operation.

The odd thing is, though, that all three of my children had an appendix out at much the same age as I was when I had mine.

Before I start to talk of the Porlock doctor, I want to say a bit more about Dr Head.

My mother thought so much of him, she trusted him implicitly. I believe that we children were not the only ones to have become neurotic. Did my mother get over anxious on our behalf?

Dr Head's version of "pink water in a tonic bottle" must have been thought up to save my mother worrying. His advice to her was to put each child that complained of any stomach trouble on to a diet of bread and hot milk and *under no circumstance* were they to have anything else until they were really better. Keep it up for three days, he advised her, and if the child is still ill bring them back to me.

There was not one of us who could keep this up, with the lovely smells of Ma's cooking all around us.

Before this ruse, he had very successfully used another with Sheila. After she had gone on many worrying expeditions to Dr Head, he gravely informed us that our sister Sheila had a floating kidney. He advised us that that there was nothing to be done about it, that she should carry on as usual, not worry and learn to live with it. He did not expect that it would get any worse, and to cheer up for goodness sake.

It was years after he had gone and Sheila found herself with some affliction requiring medical advice, that my mother went with her to see the doctor at Porlock, thinking he should be made aware of Sheila's floating kidney. Gravely he was informed of the situation and to the discomfort of them both, he howled with laughter and asked for the story to be repeated. Apparently there is no such thing as a floating kidney.

I remember Dr Head dealing with three specific cases of illnesses or accidents amongst us children. The first was Tom, when he was about five years old or younger. I was not around then, so I do not actually recall the incident, only of hearing how horrific it was. Tom had pulled over the kettle of boiling water, bubbling away on its crook above the open fire. There was a handle on this contraption, called a lazy Susan, by which you could pull the kettle forward into a pouring position. This he did and was very badly scalded from one hip all the way down his leg. Today this would be a hospital emergency. Then, the doctor came each day to dress it. It must have been extremely painful for Tom.

Margaret had a poisoned gland in her neck. After the initial visit from the doctor, she and I would set off on horseback all the way to Rockford to have it dealt with at his surgery. This was most unpleasant, unplugging the hole in her neck and replugging it before we went home. We did this for several days before it dropped down to every other day,

Sheila had one broken collarbone, Josie I think two, Tom two and had he had three that would undoubtedly have been broken as well.

At one stage I regarded my mother, Louie and Dr Head as really untrustworthy traitors. This was when I got pleurisy, when I was perhaps four or five years old. I remember getting lots of attention (at last!) and not feeling anything but happy. I recall my mother putting out the small silver spirit stove, which had a little gallery around the top, and filling it with methylated spirit. When asked what it was to be used for, she said, "Oh, it's just for the doctor to heat something up."

I was lying on my mother's side of their big double bed, which was unusual, because I had been taken from my own bed a day or two before and fitted, just, into a cot.

I was aware of a soft buzz of conversation with the doctor in the room and the plop, plop, plop of whatever was cooking in the small pan on the stove.

Dr Head remarked to my mother that perhaps another pair of hands might be useful, so Louie was called up to the room, which added to my happiness at being the centre of attention.

My mother said, "The doctor wants you to turn on to your stomach, he's going to put a plaster on your back." And, to this day, I believe she added, "It won't hurt a bit." So I was held down while this boiling antiphlogistin (see how the name is branded on my brain!) plaster was placed on my back.

After Josie was born, Dr Head had told my mother she should have no more children. Each of us had been born at home. Three years later she was pregnant with Sheila. A few years after Sheila was born we came back from school one day to find a very sober group of grown ups.

My father said, "Your mother's got to go into hospital for an operation."

This was startling news for us all. Hospital ... we at once saw the seriousness of this. No one went into hospital, except to die.

"I will be gone for some time, maybe weeks," she said.

I asked, "Is it cancer?"

Immediately my father crossed the room and gave me a sharp clip on the ear. Cancer was not a word to be bandied about in those days.

My mother went into hospital almost at once and had a hysterectomy.

She was away for a long time.

1944 Molly.

Margaret in 1950.

1945 Granfer and Granny Ridd.

Mother in 1969.

Sheila, David Tucker and Aunt Edith, New Zealand, 1956.

THE WEATHER IN THE HILLS

WE SEEMED to get more fog in the hills then. I remember some really thick ones when you could not see across our then very small fields. I remember too what it did to sound, often being able to hear Bert or Bob French talking to each other in the fields at Yenworthy, or, being in the right Broomstreet fields, hearing voices from Silcombe.

If there was a sea fog then we were in the clear and could look down on the sea of rolling white mist, sometimes so beautiful, so dramatic, it took your breath away.

What we did get more of was snow. Each winter great drifts of the stuff blocked our lane, keeping us prisoners for weeks on end. This winter there have been only two occasions when I found it wisest not to go down to the farm, and that was mainly because I felt that I might be trapped there, even though the snow was minimal. Old memories die hard.

Those of us whose job it was to see to the livestock had a very exhausting time in deep snow: simply getting around was hard enough but miles had to walked sometimes just to locate the sheep, trying to fathom out where and under which hedge some of the flock might be buried. Then came the business of digging them out and it was amazing to see them brought out, not looking much the worse for wear even after several days.

Now they needed extra feed and, with every field covered in snow and not a bit of greenery to be seen, it was out with the hay, the cake and the roots.

The cows that were housed in bad weather were easier to feed, but the ones on Porlock common were a different matter. On a few occasions more recently, hay has been dropped by helicopter, but in those days, if the roads were quite impassable, it was serious for the Exmoor ponies and any cattle out on the moor, although they could get some sustenance from wind-blown areas where the heather was more exposed.

Rainfall in the hills has always been high, and yet farmers of old seemed to anticipate drought more than we do today. David says that he remembers eight ponds on Broomstreet, one or two being necessary for the water wheel and the rest being for watering the meads. I do recall my father saying that, as it was so dry, we had better "let go" the ponds. The water then ran through channels across the top of the meads and was breached at intervals to run down and water the meads.

Wild, windy weather was another matter. Once I walked all the way to Porlock in a howling gale despite my mother's protests, because I had arranged to spend the night with a school friend.

All was well until my friend Pat and her sister Bridget fell out over whether their tortoise should stay in its box because of the awful weather or be put out on the lawn. Pat said out, Bridget said in. I sided with Bridget, we fell out and I became so angry that I collected my stuff and walked back all the way home.

Imagine the distress this caused Pat's parents. The weather was foul and there was no getting to tell my parents that I had left, because we did not have a phone at Broomstreet.

The truth was I loved being out in a gale and I arrived home just before dark much to everyone's surprise.

SHEEP SHEARING

JUNE WAS the sheep-shearing month, weather permitting and men being available. Granny Ridd's diary for 1899 tells of the farms included in their shearing rota. From Saturday June 10th, through to Friday June 23rd, they sheared at eleven farms: Buscombe, Lynn, Ashton, Wingate, Broomstreet, Hall, Yenworthy, Farley, Kipscombe, West Ilkerton and Hallslake.

The closeness of the people on the shearing list is apparent, in that most of the family went to most of the venues.

Another interesting entry concerns the sending of the previous year's wool to Minehead. "Nine carts, two from Broomstreet, two from Wingate, two from Kipscombe. One each from Lynn, Hallslake and Yenworthy."

In those days of "muck from the midden", a small amount of lime and (according to brother David) the odd cartload of guano, to spread on the fields, the stocking capacity for a hill farm was about two sheep or one cow to an acre. Hence the comparatively small amount of wool.

I like to imagine those nine carts with high lades (the ladder-like framework fixed to the front and back of carts to increase the amount they could carry), making the journey from Countisbury to Minehead along unmade roads. I visualise them trundling steadily along, all in a row, raising a dust seen on the skyline, as they come along Whitstones. I feel for the stumbling horses, with their heavy load, as they descend Porlock Hill.

And I can see them trudging slowly back in the dusk, the carts empty, skeletal, etched across the sky.

When I was a youngster in the 1930s, little had changed. We had to work together with other farmers, as all the men from one farm would come to your place and then, when the job was done, you went to their farm until all the sheep in the neighbourhood had been shorn.

Working together on this most important business of sheep shearing, many of us waiting for the wool cheque to pay our bills, created a traditional rota. The first Monday after something or other became Farmer Herbert's day and so on.

However, the whole thing could be thrown into disarray by too much rain at the wrong time. Wet fleeces are definitely no good.

There were two things about sheep shearing that I never quite under-stood as a child. Why were the shearing clothes always white? It seemed so impractical: each day a clean white jacket and trousers in the traditional roll, which held the sharp shears safely. I could understand the roll; it went over the shoulders, convenient for those who came on horseback. I suppose, too, sheep mess would show up more on white. Many farming household in those days were fastidiously clean. If necessary, the jacket or trousers could be easily removed before sitting down to a meal.

The other thing that puzzled me was the barrel of water and ferns outside the door for the men to wash in before coming in to eat. It turns out that this mixture was better than the soap of the day for ridding the hands of sheep grease, otherwise known as lanolin, and its strong sheep smell.

Before shearing began, Grannie Richards would come to brew the beer. She did not come too early, lest my father drank it all before the start of shearing. Open barrels, that is barrels cut in half, were spread about the wash house and held mysterious brown mixtures, fluffy bits of barm floating on the surface. That smell, I suppose it was the hops, was so good. Even now, whenever I pass a brewery, I think of Grannie and her beer.

Other jobs for the men to do in preparation for the shearing making temporary pens for holding the sheep, with easy access for the catcher; gathering ferns or bracken to put in these pens to stop the fleeces getting dirty; and forming a holding area with hurdles for the fleeces. The barn had to be swept clean, for the price obtained for the wool was affected by its condition.

A space had to be made for the sheep marker, usually the owner, with enough room for the brazier and the large tin of marking paint. It was common to brand each sheep on its horn, as well as the paint marking on its back. Space was also needed for the sheep to be handled, one at a time, as they were shorn. Any sheep running amok amongst this mixture of fire and paint would have presented a serious problem.

After being branded, the sheep would be released with access into a field. You would have thought that such joyous freedom after the harrowing shearing and branding, and not having any food for several hours, would have been appreciated. But no, not until lambs had found their mothers and mothers their lambs would there be any peace. I loved watching their puzzled expressions, their disbelief and suspicion, as each saw the other all shaven and shorn. Then came that particular bleat, as they recognised a particular smell, and the pair of them would run off up to the field.

There was much to do indoors too. There were perhaps as many as twelve men to feed three times a day, with dinner (lunch to you), tea and supper. Children and women fed themselves later. Dinner was always a hot meal, often a home cured ham, home-grown kale, potatoes, swede mashed with cream, and parsley sauce. Tea would be farmhouse cake, cream, scones, and always bread and butter. Supper consisted of cold ham, pickles, beetroot and salad with Exmoor dressing, followed by trifle and cheese. The pudding for dinner was nearly always a pie made with gooseberries from the garden. I well remember the hours spent topping and tailing for so many people. You should understand that shearing at some farms took three or four days, according to how much help they were able to get.

To say that we were very pleased when it was all over is a bit of an understatement.

All through the day at roughly hourly intervals my sister or I would be sent round with the beer jug. The good beer was both food and drink; each man took only a few swigs, mostly to replace lost moisture from all that sweating.

After supper on the last day, when the last sheep had been shorn, people began to relax, pipes were lit and beer passed around more copiously. Old songs were sung, healths drunk and stories told. They seemed to me always old stories that I had heard before, but that didn't matter in the least. There was a lot of laughter and a good feeling before they picked up their rolls of shearing clothes, got on their horses and rode off into the night.

PONY GATHERING

WHEN I was quite young, the annual pony gathering took place on the moor. This practice died out very soon for us at Broomstreet as it became uneconomic.

Yet I have a distinct memory of a great herd of wild ponies being driven with much shouting and hollering, pounding their small unshod hooves across the heather and, eventually, down our lane.

First the ponies had to be rounded up from their quiet grazing in the goyals and combes and from the hilltops, by men on horseback. It was a noisy business, trying to get them into any sort of order. Galloping and splashing up hill and down, they were corralled into the pound, whinnying and milling around whilst the gatherers had lunch before sorting them out.

Manoeuvred into our enclosed yard, terrified and flinging themselves at any seeming way of escape, however futile, they would leap and charge.

From such a frantic crowd, mares and matching foals had to be sorted and branded. Nothing would convince me that the branding was not cruel: the smell of burning flesh and, yes, the quick recovery, made it all pretty grim to watch.

That same day or the next those ponies not being taken to Bampton Fair or Brendon pony sale were back again on the hills.

As the pony gathering was, to my mind, one of the most dramatic and colourful of Exmoor farming life, putting it into words for me is difficult. Certainly when I read Hope Bourne's account of the gathering in her book, *Living on Exmoor*, I do not feel qualified to even try. If you want to read it for yourself, look in the chapter headed *October*.

VILLAGE HALLS

HARVEST HOMES, the festival for the end of harvest, took place in the village hall. Trestle tables lined the sides and filled the middle of the room. A posse of local wives would have spent the afternoon decking the tables with white cloths and setting them with glasses, cutlery and little posies of late flowers. All were welcomed.

Everyone knew everyone, so it would have been much the same mix as if you had had the party in any friend's house or your own.

The room would be full of happy relaxed people, all of us speaking the same warm Devonshire dialect. We children from remote farms, finding so many of our friends in a different from school environment, were happy and excited.

Those meals were so good. There was usually rare beef, served with plenty of fresh vegetables, Yorkshire pudding and all the trimmings, followed by apple pie and loads of cream, cheeses and lots of beer for the men, with a few discreet sherries for the women.

After the meal there would be some dancing, lots of talk and a table or two of card playing – everything going on at once. We all went home happy in the strength of our common bond – at least for the time being!

At Christmas, the party for children was the highlight of the year. The hall was beautifully decorated with balloons, holly and mistletoe, and the tea table laden with jellies, cakes and sandwiches. Most important of all, at the top of the room stood the huge Christmas tree, decorated with unlit candles, waiting for us all to finish eating. Spurred on by the prospect, especially the agonising wonder at which of the gaudily wrapped parcels was to be ours, we soon demolished our tea.

The candles would be lit and, perfectly timed, there would sound a loud rapping at the door. Adults all around us looked scared, asking us who we thought it might be. Then Father Christmas entered the room.

How we watched each other as the names were called out, seeing each child feverishly trying to remove the wrapping from their present. One year I got a lovely large doll, which was not greatly appreciated by me. Somehow in our family there was not a history of being part of a doll owning society. However, I was determined to do the right thing by her, until Tom and I found some weeks later that, if shaken, the doll would rattle. We wondered what might be causing this sound, and Tom duly came up with the idea that it might be a diamond. In two shakes of a lamb's tail we had her head off. I do not remember any grieving after her beheading: if anything it was almost a relief. Back to the party, I loved and feared the games. One we called Truckle the Trencher, otherwise known as Forfeits. Spinning the wooden trencher, in this case a bread board, the person called to spin it would wait until it almost came to a stop before calling a name. This meant a mad rush to get to the thing or there would be a fearful forfeit to pay, often in the shape of mistletoe sprigs, doing a dance, reciting a poem or singing a song. The possibilities for torture were endless.

Oranges and Lemons was another very popular game, all of us flushed and breathless with excitement at the threat in the words we sang – "Here comes the chopper to chop off your head", then being caught and the words sung with such glee – "and the last man's dead."

There was for children a magic in village halls and there was also a belittling of the experience when we got to around eleven years old or so. It was all right for the food, but for "sophisticated" people like us not much fun really.

Village halls became popular again when we were teenagers during the war.

Jack was essential to our village hall dances. It was only occasionally that we went as far as to book a three-piece band. For the regular hops it was Jack and his accordion. I loved bouncing around to accordion playing. There were a few tunes we could rely on getting – *Daisy, Daisy* and *When I met Connie in the cornfield* – or was it *Polly in the Parlour…*?

The thing with Jack was that he had to be loudly appreciated with frequent claps and cheers after each number. If he felt that we were taking him for granted he might well just pack up and go home. He had a peculiar habit, when displeased, of sucking his teeth with a clucking sound, at the same time slightly stretching his neck sideways, before leaving in a huff.

I can see us now, pleading with him, as he strapped his accordion to his back and mounted his motorbike, a very sad and deflated bunch. He would explain the next day that if we thought he wasn't good enough, we could always ask John Ash, but if we did we must bear in mind that, "good as young John might be, he can't vamp, no, that's one thing he'll never be able to do is vamp." We had to agree with him, even though we had no idea what vamping was.

Jack was widowed and lived at Broomstreet farm cottage with his daughter Marjorie and his widowed father. I do not remember his ever working for us, but I suppose he must have done. I see him with a red face, a drooping moustache, a motorbike, and a great fondness for Louie. Each week he brought her a bag of pear drops, which Louie handed on to us with a sniff, remarking on his total lack of imagination and the fact that she had never liked pear drops. We did, and we hoped he wouldn't go over to something that Louie enjoyed. Nothing came of Jack's hopes, for his daughter Marjorie and Louie were much the same age and Louie in no way seemed to respond to his advances and most evenings he sat in our kitchen watching Louie at work and looking dejected.

Marjorie worked for us as a land girl. I do not recall her doing anything in the farmhouse. She was a lovely warm person and had a lot to put up with, as we children were at times pretty awful. She was always cheerful and I sometimes have a rush of guilt that I did not behave very well to her.

Jack's father had a long white beard. When he wasn't sitting in the chimney corner of the cottage, drinking tea, he would wander round his garden talking to his Rhode Island Reds and searching the hedges round his garden looking for stolen nests. If he should find one he went in search of the culprit saying, over and over, "Ooh laid egg, then? Ooh laid egg?"

We children found this hilarious: an old man talking to chickens.

During the war there was a radar station on the hill above Yearnor farm and local houses were required to billet as many airmen as possible. We had three bedrooms to spare and airmen came and went at will. I do not remember us catering for them, but perhaps we did.

I remember two from Cornwall, Bill Nute and Ed Crago, Taffy who was Welsh, and Joe, a Geordie who enthralled me when he sang the Blaydon Races, and with whom I remember falling in love at the age of fifteen, and being very upset when he brought his local girl friend up to meet us and finally married her.

They were a lovely bunch of men. Sometimes their wives or girl friends came to stay and their happiness and infectious camaraderie would permeate the whole house, even affecting my father. In the evenings great gales of laughter could be heard from all the rooms.

If this was our war effort then I enjoyed every minute – a very female point of view, I suspect.

Yet, oh, the sadness and romance of those parted lovers in the wartime songs: you could have wept for them. By the time the war ended, I was coming up to eighteen and felt a sense of guilt and of being somehow not quite worthy, because I had contributed nothing and lost no one. This mood, I regret to say, did not last long. Soon I was out partying again with the best of them.

Littlewood, now known as Twitchen, circa 1960.

Littlewood, now known as Twitchen, circa 1960.

Our Swiss friend, Margrit, standing on a five bar gate, with our dog Susie, during the snow of January 1963.

Uncle Herbert, my mother and "Uncle" Jack Woollacott in 1987.

BROOMSTREET NOW

LOOKING TO my more recent memories of family life at Broomstreet and of living in it as it is today, the turning point came when my father died in 1964.

David was the only fit member of the family living at the farm by then. Tom had, through a wildish life, broken, at different times, ankles, ribs, a leg and collarbones, and in later life suffered from osteoarthritis. He was already feeling the effect of his farmer's lung, a kind of emphysema caught from handling fusty hay in an era when no one wore masks, and it was cancer of the oesophagus that was to end his days in 2005 at the age of eighty-one.

David and Tom decided that the best thing to do was to let the grass. This was not a success, with relations and friends usually taking the same lots each year, so that it became almost unnecessary to have a grass sale. Bidders knew what they always had, and there built up an unspoken rule that no one should bid against the ones already in possession.

Once, when an intruder into this cosy arrangement dared to start to bid for a particular lot, he was informed, "Hey! You can't bid for that. John vore Yearnor always has that lot." The bidder, visibly cowed, hastily left the scene.

About 25 years ago Phyllis and Sid Coward moved into Broomstreet Cottage and immediately fitted in. David and Tom found a common bond with Sid, while Phyllis and my mother hit it off right away. I shall be always grateful to Phyllis for those last happy years of my mother's life at Broomstreet.

It took until 1994, the year my mother died, before it was decided to sell up. The important part of this was that somehow it had to be made possible for my two brothers, who had lived there all their lives, to buy the farmhouse and the land around it. It may sound odd that the actual farmhouse had to go into the sale, but that was a legal necessity.

Most happily for us the land went in lots to our local friends and two cousins, people we knew who would farm it much as my brothers would have liked to have done, who could talk the talk, and not to people, as my mother would have said, "from away". And David and Tom were able to stay on in the farmhouse and surrounding fields.

FINALE

MANY TIMES, during this past winter while I have been putting together these memories of mine, I have wondered as to what interest they can be to anyone and often thought of shelving them. My reasons for carrying on are several.

Firstly, this trawling of my past has helped belatedly to lay a few ghosts, especially regarding my father. His instincts were good, I believe, but he was inadequate as a father and a husband. Now I feel no more than a great sadness that he and we missed any chance of closeness. The price for us all was too high, especially for my mother.

Secondly, I think that by delving into my memories and writing them down – which was not always easy – I might well have postponed serious senility for a bit!

Thirdly, it seems an opportunity to let members of the family know how much they were appreciated, which is not the sort of thing we are good at saying to each other.

A few weeks ago, the snow was too bad to risk the farm lane, so I drove along to County Gate and, looking out at the wonderful snowy landscape, spent some time thinking about our lives at Broomstreet. I thought a lot about Sheila and the guts it took to go alone to New Zealand. We all miss her and her family, but I am happy for them and a little envious too. Inside, I just feel, "Good on ya, Sheila."

Thinking back to those far-off days, when we went to school at Oare and of the physical effort required for young children to get there, it seems to me that so much more could be achieved then, because it was the norm. Having said that, though, my granddaughter, at the age of five, recently walked with her parents to the top of Snowdon, starting at two in the afternoon and getting back at ten.

There was so much more bird life then. In May and June, we heard cuckoos each and every day, and by early June there were families of buzzards overhead. The Challacombe Horniwig, as we called the peewit, lifted off from the fields in great flocks of noise. And thrushes were commonplace.

We now have fewer rabbits, which accounts for there being fewer buzzards and fewer foxes. I recently saw two rabbits at Broomstreet, where once there would have been hundreds. But this change is certainly only temporary. Two rabbits can easily become two hundred in two years' time...

Today, pulling in to look down on Porlock Bay, I see many things to delight in. A lonely gull is standing in the snow, waiting for picnic scraps. But this is no picnic weather. The three other cars are empty, their owners gone walkabout in this beautiful landscape.

A curtain of heavy snow droops across the channel, approaching slowly.

The hills of Wales are streaked with snow.

A shaft of early sun beats at the window.

My car is suddenly surrounded by eight Exmoor ponies. They paw at the frozen puddles with dainty feet, to drink the muddied water. Then, with a joyous leap and a gallop, off they go over the hill.

The optimistic gull, buffeted by cold winds, stands its ground, waiting.

And I am full of gratitude for such a fortunate life.